Coffee With God!

Daily Devotional

"Behold, I stand at the door and knock: if any man hear my voice and open the door, I will come in to him, and will sup with him, and he with me." (Revelation 3:20, ASV)

Harrison Sharma Mungal, Ph.D., PsyD.

Coffee With God!

2025

Copyright © Harrison S. Mungal

All rights reserved. Neither this publication nor any part of this publication may be reproduced or transmitted in any form or by any means, electronic or mechanical, including photocopying, recording or any information storage and retrieval system, without permission in writing from the author.

Unless otherwise identified, Scripture quotations are from

New King James Version of the Bible.

Contact author via email:
hsmungal@hotmail.com
info@agetoage.ca
www.agetoage.ca
www.harrisonmungal.com
www.harrisonmungalbooks.com
Facebook: Harrison Mungal
Twitter: AgeToAgeInc1
LinkedIn: Harrison Mungal, Ph.D., PsyD
YouTube: Harrison Mungal
Phone: 905-533-1334

ABOUT *the* AUTHOR

Harrison Sharma Mungal,
BTh, MCC, MSW, PhD, PsyD

Dr. Mungal is a devoted therapist with a background in mental health and clinical psychology, driven by a genuine passion for life and the well-being of those under his care. With an impressive literary portfolio comprising over 40 books and a seasoned public speaking career that has reached audiences in over 42 nations, he brings a wealth of knowledge and skills to his practice.

Alongside his professional accomplishments, Dr. Mungal places a high value on family, with a successful marriage of over 34 years, seven children, and multiple grandchildren. In addition to his clinical practice, Dr. Mungal and his wife have played pivotal roles in church planting, pastoral ministry, and missionary work, even during the challenging times of the Cold War in Croatia from 1994-1997. They have nurtured congregations, established churches, and served as missionaries, demonstrating a deep commitment to spreading the gospel. Their dedication extended to running a Bible college, Metro Bible College, for over a decade before transitioning into mental health and addictions counselling.

Dr. Mungal is widely respected for his unique ability to blend biblical principles with scientific insights, adding a distinctive "psychology twist" to his therapeutic approach. He explained God made us Body, Soul (mind, will and emotions) and Spirit. As much as people need support physically and spiritually, "the soul is where people are wounded and is in need of healing." His expertise has been sought after by various media outlets, including appearances on television programs including 700 Clubs Canada and 100 Huntly St. He has also been invited to speak at prestigious institutions such as the Attorney General of Canada, police departments, hospitals, community agencies, and churches. His contributions have earned him accolades and recognition from local authorities, police departments, mayors, community leaders, and countless families.

With over 21 years of experience in mental health, psychiatry, and psychology, coupled with over four decades dedicated to teaching and preaching the gospel, Dr. Mungal possesses a wealth of expertise in both fields. His educational background is equally impressive, with a Christian Leadership Certificate, a Ministerial Diploma from two years of Bible College, a bachelor's degree in Theology, two master's degrees (in Counselling and Social Work), and two doctorate degrees (in Social Work and Clinical Psychology).

In summary, Dr. Mungal's journey is a testament to his unwavering commitment to serving others, integrating his faith with his professional expertise to make a positive impact in the lives of countless individuals, couples, and families. His multifaceted career reflects a deep sense of purpose and a profound dedication to promoting holistic healing and spiritual growth.

TABLE *of* CONTENTS

ABOUT the AUTHOR .... **Error! Bookmark not defined.**
Week 1 Monday 16
Week 1 Wednesday 17
Week 1 Thursday 19
Week 1 Friday 20
Week 2 Monday 21
Week 2 Tuesday 21
Week 2 Wednesday 22
Week 2 Thursday 23
Week 2 Friday 24
Week 3 Monday 25
Week 3 Tuesday 26
Week 3 Wednesday 27
Week 3 Thursday 28
Week 3 Friday 29
Week 4 Monday 30
Week 4 Tuesday 31

Week 4 Wednesday 32

Week 4 Thursday 33

Week 4 Friday 34

Week 5 Monday 35

Week 5 Tuesday 36

Week 5 Wednesday 37

Week 5 Thursday 38

Week 5 Friday 39

Week 6 Monday 40

Week 6 Tuesday 41

Week 6 Wednesday 42

Week 6 Thursday 43

Week 6 Friday 45

Week 7 Monday 45

Week 7 Tuesday 46

Week 7 Wednesday 47

Week 7 Thursday 49

Week 7 Friday 49

Week 8 Monday 50

Week 8 Tuesday 51

Week 8 Wednesday 52

Week 8 Thursday 54

Week 8 Friday 54

Week 9 Monday 55

Week 9 Tuesday 56

Week 9 Wednesday 57

Week 9 Thursday 58

- Week 9 Friday 60
- Week 10 Monday 60
- Week 10 Tuesday 62
- Week 10 Wednesday 62
- Week 10 Thursday 63
- Week 10 Friday 65
- Week 11 Monday 65
- Week 11 Tuesday 66
- Week 11 Wednesday 67
- Week 11 Thursday 69
- Week 11 Friday 69
- Week 12 Monday 70
- Week 12 Tuesday 71
- Week 12 Wednesday 72
- Week 12 Thursday 73
- Week 12 Friday 74
- Week 13 Monday 76
- Week 13 Tuesday 76
- Week 13 Wednesday 77
- Week 13 Thursday 78
- Week 13 Friday 79
- Week 14 Monday 80
- Week 14 Tuesday 81
- Week 14 Wednesday 83
- Week 14 Thursday 83
- Week 14 Friday 84
- Week 15 Monday 85

Week 15 Tuesday 86
Week 15 Wednesday 87
Week 15 Thursday 88
Week 15 Friday 89
Week 16 Monday 90
Week 16 Tuesday 91
Week 16 Wednesday 92
Week 16 Thursday 93
Week 16 Friday 94
Week 17 Monday 95
Week 17 Tuesday 96
Week 17 Wednesday 97
Week 17 Thursday 98
Week 17 Friday 99
Week 18 Monday 100
Week 18 Tuesday 101
Week 18 Wednesday 102
Week 18 Thursday 103
Week 18 Friday 104
Week 19 Monday 105
Week 19 Tuesday 106
Week 19 Wednesday 107
Week 19 Thursday 108
Week 19 Friday 109
Week 20 Monday 110
Week 20 Tuesday 111
Week 20 Wednesday 112

Week 20 Thursday 113

Week 20 Friday 114

Week 21 Monday 115

Week 21 Tuesday 116

Week 21 Wednesday 118

Week 21 Thursday 118

Week 21 Friday 119

Week 22 Monday 120

Week 22 Tuesday 121

Week 22 Wednesday 122

Week 22 Thursday 124

Week 22 Friday 124

Week 23 Monday 125

Week 23 Tuesday 126

Week 23 Wednesday 127

Week 23 Thursday 128

Week 23 Friday .... **Error! Bookmark not defined.**

Week 24 Monday 130

Week 24 Tuesday 131

Week 24 Wednesday 133

Week 24 Thursday 133

Week 24 Friday 134

Week 25 Monday 135

Week 25 Tuesday 136

Week 25 Wednesday 137

Week 25 Thursday 139

Week 25 Friday 139

Week 26 Monday	140
Week 26 Tuesday	141
Week 26 Wednesday	142
Week 26 Thursday	143
Week 26 Friday	144
Week 27 Monday	145
Week 27 Tuesday	146
Week 27 Wednesday	148
Week 27 Thursday	148
Week 27 Friday	149
Week 28 Monday	151
Week 28 Tuesday	151
Week 28 Wednesday	152
Week 28 Thursday	154
Week 28 Friday	154
Week 29 Monday	155
Week 29 Tuesday	156
Week 29 Wednesday	157
Week 29 Thursday	158
Week 29 Friday	159
Week 30 Monday	160
Week 30 Tuesday	161
Week 30 Wednesday	162
Week 30 Thursday	164
Week 30 Friday	164
Week 31 Monday	165
Week 31 Tuesday	166

Week 31 Wednesday	167
Week 31 Thursday	169
Week 31 Friday	169
Week 32 Monday	170
Week 32 Tuesday	171
Week 32 Wednesday	172
Week 32 Thursday	173
Week 32 Friday	174
Week 33 Monday	175
Week 33 Tuesday	176
Week 33 Wednesday	178
Week 33 Thursday	179
Week 33 Friday	180
Week 34 Monday	180
Week 34 Tuesday	181
Week 34 Wednesday	182
Week 34 Thursday	183
Week 34 Friday	184
Week 35 Monday	185
Week 35 Tuesday	186
Week 35 Wednesday	187
Week 35 Thursday	188
Week 35 Friday	190
Week 36 Monday	190
Week 36 Tuesday	191
Week 36 Wednesday	192
Week 36 Thursday	193

Week 36 Friday 194
Week 37 Monday 195
Week 37 Tuesday 196
Week 37 Wednesday 197
Week 37 Thursday 198
Week 37 Friday 199
Week 38 Monday 200
Week 38 Tuesday 201
Week 38 Wednesday 202
Week 38 Thursday 203
Week 38 Friday 204
Week 39 Monday 205
Week 39 Tuesday 206
Week 39 Wednesday 207
Week 39 Thursday 208
Week 39 Friday 209
Week 40 Monday 210
Week 40 Tuesday 211
Week 40 Wednesday 212
Week 40 Thursday 213
Week 40 Friday 214
Week 41 Monday 215
Week 41 Tuesday 216
Week 41 Wednesday 217
Week 41 Thursday 218
Week 41 Friday 219
Week 42 Monday 220

Week 42 Tuesday	221
Week 42 Wednesday	222
Week 42 Thursday	223
Week 42 Friday	224
Week 43 Monday	225
Week 43 Tuesday	226
Week 43 Wednesday	227
Week 43 Thursday	228
Week 43 Friday	229
Week 44 Monday	230
Week 44 Tuesday	231
Week 44 Wednesday	232
Week 44 Thursday	233
Week 44 Friday	234
Week 45 Monday	235
Week 45 Tuesday	237
Week 45 Wednesday	238
Week 45 Thursday	238
Week 45 Friday	239
Week 46 Monday	240
Week 46 Tuesday	241
Week 46 Wednesday	242
Week 46 Thursday	243
Week 46 Friday	244
Week 47 Monday	245
Week 47 Tuesday	246
Week 47 Wednesday	247

Week 47 Thursday	249
Week 47 Friday	249
Week 48 Monday	250
Week 48 Tuesday	251
Week 48 Wednesday	252
Week 48 Friday	254
Week 49 Monday	255
Week 49 Tuesday	256
Week 49 Wednesday	257
Week 49 Thursday	259
Week 49 Friday	259
Week 50 Monday	260
Week 50 Tuesday	262
Week 50 Wednesday	262
Week 50 Thursday	263
Week 50 Friday	264
Week 51 Monday	265
Week 51 Tuesday	266
Week 51 Wednesday	268
Week 51 Thursday	268
Week 51 Friday	269
Week 52 Monday	271
Week 52 Tuesday	271
Week 52 Wednesday	272
Week 52 Thursday	273
Week 52 Friday	275

Coffee With God!

Week 1 Monday

You Are A Hero!

The angel of the LORD appeared to him and said, "Mighty hero, the LORD is with you!" (Judges 6:12, NLT)

Growing up, we were taught to address others with respect, using titles like "sir," "ma'am," "mister," and "lady." We called our parents "papi" and "mami," and had special names for them based on our culture and language. These forms of address weren't just about politeness—they were about recognizing the important roles these individuals played in our lives.

In scripture, the Angel of the Lord called Gideon a "mighty hero" because that is how God saw him. This wasn't just a name; it was a reflection of his true potential and strength in God's eyes. God sees us in the same way. He views us as His heroes and champions, and speaks of us with pride in heaven as we strive to obey and follow His commands.

It's easy to undervalue ourselves, but we must remember the greatness within us: we carry the salvation of the Lord, His way, and His truth. We are not just ordinary individuals; we are extraordinary in the eyes of God.

Today, I encourage you to see yourself as the hero God sees you to be. Embrace your worth, live with purpose, act with conviction, and stand your ground with the courage and confidence of a true hero. You are valued, you are strong, and you are loved. Live your life in a way that reflects this divine truth.

Week 1 Tuesday

What Your're Leaving?

"A good man leaves an inheritance to his children's children, but the sinner's wealth is laid up for the righteous."
(Proverbs 13:22, ESV)

We are raised with a mindset focused on going to school, working, entering a relationship, starting a family, retiring, and saving for both the future and unforeseen challenges. Along with this comes the idea of leaving an inheritance for our children and grandchildren. But the real question is, what are we doing now to leave something meaningful behind? What kind of legacy are we creating?

I often wish I had the knowledge in my twenties and thirties that I possess now. It's essential to understand that life isn't just about ourselves; it's about the others whom God blesses us with, akin to the inheritance of our bloodline. Once we grasp this, we realize that the wealth of the sinners is laid up for us, enabling us to establish a legacy of blessings for our children and future generations. Many of today's wealthy individuals bear well-known names and are firmly established thanks to the foundations laid by their parents or grandparents. God desires to give you more than you can imagine so that you can leave a lasting legacy. Receive the blessings today wholeheartedly for tomorrow's generation!

Week 1 Wednesday

You Are Being Carried!

"There you saw how the LORD your God carried you, as a father carries his son, all the way you went until you reached this place." (Deuteronomy 1:31, NIV)

As I read this scripture, memories of raising my seven children flood my mind. Raising six daughters and one son demanded an incredible amount of energy, time, and effort. I often found myself carrying them in my arms during our walks, especially when they were tired and needed to rest. I would hold them on my arms, my back, and my neck, embracing and protecting them so they wouldn't feel the exhaustion I was experiencing.

Kathleen and I always made sure to have snacks, food, and water ready when they were hungry. Wow, wow, wow. This is how God carried the Israelites in the wilderness, and it's how He carries us today. God provides, protects, and preserves us in His arms as He leads us on this journey. He ensures that we endure and does whatever it takes to ease our pain when we feel tired and tempted to give up.

In His arms, He holds us tightly, shielding us from anything and anyone that might try to harm us. Today, see yourself in the arms of a mighty God who cares for you, carrying you through every challenge and triumph.

God's embrace is always there, lifting us up when we are weary and offering comfort when we are in need. Just as I carried my children, God carries us, offering His strength and love to get us through even the toughest times. Embrace this truth and feel His presence in every step of your journey.

Week 1 Thursday

 Soul Care

"Beloved, I pray that you may prosper in all things and be in health, just as your soul prospers." (3 John 2, NKJV)

When I was working in the Emergency Department at the hospital, each 12-hour shift was filled with individuals experiencing both physical and mental illness. Their emotions and feelings deeply impacted their thoughts, especially when faced with a terminal diagnosis. This often led to fear, worry, anger, and bitterness, which can poison the soul. Such negativity disrupts our sleep, eating habits, concentration, and memory.

I've seen firsthand how these emotions can take a toll on a person's overall well-being. But God's plan is for us to be healthy in body, soul, and spirit. When our soul prospers, it alleviates the stress that contributes to medical and psychiatric issues, and it removes the poison that gradually erodes the joy in our hearts.

Soul care is incredibly important. It's not just about managing our physical health but nurturing our inner selves as well. Taking time to care for your soul can reset your mind, bringing peace and clarity. Whether it's through prayer, meditation, spending time in nature, or simply taking a moment to breathe deeply, these acts of soul care are vital.

Today, I encourage you to make a conscious effort to care for your soul. Reflect on what brings you peace and joy, and embrace those practices. Remember, a healthy soul reduces stress and fosters a healthier, happier life. Take some time today to nourish your soul and reset your mind. You deserve it.

Week 1 Friday

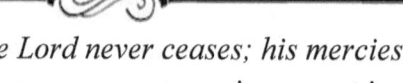 New Mercy!

"The steadfast love of the Lord never ceases; his mercies never come to an end; they are new every morning; great is your faithfulness" (Lamentations 3:22-23-ESV).

What a wonderful reminder it is that God's love for us is truly unending. He constantly loves us, hoping we'll make the right choices to live according to His will. And when we falter, His mercy is renewed every morning, offering us another chance to learn from our past mistakes and move forward with grace.

I often find myself wrestling with weaknesses that can sometimes feel overwhelming. It's in these moments that I realize how crucial it is to stop being so hard on myself. We all carry the unnecessary burden of self-criticism, which only hinders us from fulfilling God's beautiful plan for our lives.

God wants us to embrace His fresh mercy each day. Each morning, we have the opportunity to reset, to let go of yesterday's failures, and to make the changes needed to move forward on the right path. It's not about being perfect, but about being willing to grow and change.

God's mercy is new every morning, and He is steadfast in His promises and love for us. This love is a gentle reminder that we are never alone, that we are always cared for, and that we have endless opportunities to start anew. So today, let's choose to embrace God's mercy, to forgive ourselves, and to walk confidently in His love. Remember, you are deeply loved, and each day is a fresh start filled with His grace.

Week 2 Monday

Shifting The Nobodies

"Isn't it obvious that God deliberately chose men and women that the culture overlooks and exploits and abuses, chose these "nobodies" to expose the hollow pretensions of the "somebodies"? (1 Corinthians 1:27, MSG)

Growing up, I often saw myself as insignificant. My skin color, background, shortcomings, introverted nature, lack of skills, and lack of education—all these made me feel limited. My dreams were merely a way to comfort myself, imagining a happiness that seemed unattainable. However, when I encountered the God of the universe, everything changed.

I realized that it was He who had placed those dreams in my heart and orchestrated my life to bring them to fruition. Through His guidance, I gained training, experiences, education, and skills, transforming my life into someone of value and worth. The scripture says God "chose these 'nobodies' to expose the hollow pretensions of the 'somebodies.'" This verse resonates deeply with me because I have experienced this transformation firsthand.

God has taken me from feeling like a nobody to understanding my worth. He sees immense value in each of us, no matter our backgrounds or past limitations. It's His grace and love that qualify us, not our achievements or abilities. He is doing the same for you, working in your life to bring your dreams to fruition and to reveal your true worth.

Remember, you are not defined by your past or your perceived shortcomings. God has a plan for you, and He sees you as valuable. and worthy.

Week 2 Tuesday

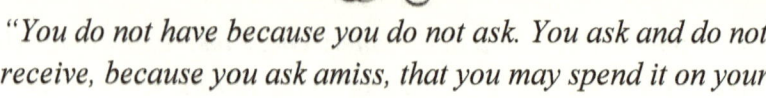
Don't Limit Your Asking

"You do not have because you do not ask. You ask and do not receive, because you ask amiss, that you may spend it on your pleasures." (James 4:2–3, NKJV)

Every time I read the scripture about asking, I'm reminded that God never sets limits on what we can ask for. In Matthew 7:7, Jesus says, "Ask, and it will be given to you; seek, and you will find; knock, and it will be opened to you." The enemy tries to make us believe there are limits, discouraging us from asking for big or seemingly impossible things. But God encourages us to ask boldly.

James tells us that we often do not receive because we do not ask. And when we ask and do not receive, it might be because our motives are not pure, seeking to fulfill our own desires. But God does not limit what we can ask for; we impose those limits on ourselves. If we ask with pure intentions and not for selfish gain, we can ask for anything: healing, financial breakthroughs, reconciliation with our children, restored relationships, strength in marital struggles, job promotions, success in exams—whatever it may be.

Take a moment to write down your prayer needs, track what you are asking for, and witness how God can accomplish the impossible. He sees immense value in your life and wants to bless you abundantly. Embrace His love and guidance, and dare to ask without limits. You are not insignificant; you are cherished and valued beyond measure. Remove the limits on your asking, and open your heart to the limitless possibilities that God offers.

Week 2 Wednesday

God Never Forgets

"God remembered Rachel; he listened to her and enabled her to conceive." (Genesis 30:22, NIV)

Rachel longed for children, but she was unable to conceive. Year after year, she watched her sister Leah having children, which deepened her frustration and discouragement. Rachel struggled to see herself ever getting pregnant. Yet, the scripture tells us, "God remembered Rachel." It wasn't about Rachel remembering God, but rather God remembering her.

Many of us feel disheartened when our prayers seem unanswered, especially when they are the promises of God. We might start to lose hope and doubt if our desires will ever come to fruition. But God's timing is perfect. He never forgets His promises. 2 Corinthians 1:20 reminds us that all His promises are "yes" and "amen." This means that what He has promised, He will surely fulfill.

Rachel's story is a powerful reminder to keep believing and trusting in the Lord. Despite the delays and disappointments, God remembered Rachel and blessed her with children. He will do the same for us. Our prayers are not forgotten; our hopes are not in vain. God's faithfulness ensures that He will bring to reality what He has promised.

So, hold on to your faith. Keep praying, keep trusting, and keep believing. Just as God remembered Rachel, He remembers you. Your desires, your prayers, and your dreams are in His heart. In His perfect time, He will bring them to pass. Trust in His promises and know that He is faithful to fulfill them.

Week 2 Thursday

Prepare Yourself!

"King Jotham became powerful because he was careful to live in obedience to the LORD his God." (2 Chronicles 27:6, NLT)

Each of us has a spirit that will one day return to God, and the choices we make in this life determine our eternal destiny. While our bodies will decay, our spirits are guided by God, who desires us to fulfill the destiny He has planned for us. When we align our lives with His will, we experience His goodness and prosperity.

Just as Jotham prepared himself to live according to the Lord's ways, we too must prepare our hearts and minds to follow God's guidance. His plans for us are far greater than anything we could dream or imagine. He has blessings, positive influences, and promotions in store for our success. God did not create us to fail; even when we feel unqualified, He has already qualified us.

Our heart's desire should be to live in obedience to the Lord, diligently seeking to align our actions with His will. As we strive for this, we will witness God's goodness pursuing us. His blessings will follow us, and we will see His hand at work in our lives.

Remember, God's plan for you is filled with hope and a future. Embrace His guidance, trust in His promises, and be diligent in your walk with Him. You are not alone; God is with you, preparing you for the incredible destiny He has set before you. Live with the assurance that His goodness and mercy will follow you all the days of your life.

Week 2 Friday

God's Vision Of Us!

"Even before he made the world, God loved us and chose us in Christ to be holy and without fault in his eyes." (Ephesians 1:4, NLT)

Before we drew our first breath, God set His heart on loving us. Even in our yet-unformed state, He cherished us with a love so profound it defies human understanding. Through Jesus Christ, He holds a radiant hope for us: that we will stand before Him, holy and without blemish. Our journey is a work in progress. We stumble, make wrong choices, and find ourselves entangled in mistakes. There are moments we are not proud of, times when our actions seem to betray the goodness within us.

The enemy seizes these moments, using our weaknesses to ensnare us in guilt, worthlessness, and shame. He whispers lies that tell us we are unworthy of love, unworthy of grace. Yet, God's vision of us remains unshaken. In His eyes, we are faultless. He looks at us not with disappointment, but with hope—a hope that we will turn from our negative choices and find our way back to Him.

God's love for us is unconditional, an unending river that flows despite our failings. He knows our hearts and sees the potential within us, always ready to embrace us with open arms. His love is a constant reminder that no matter how far we stray, we can always return to Him. His grace is sufficient, and His mercy is new every morning. Trust in His unwavering love and let it guide you back to His embrace. You are cherished, you are loved, and you are His.

Week 3 Monday

Emotional Wounds!

"Remember the wonders he has performed, his miracles, and the rulings he has given." (1 Chronicles 16:12, NLT)

We are living in a time when we are becoming more educated about our feelings and emotions. This increased understanding helps us better address emotional wounds and negative thoughts that affect our feelings. However, we can still be triggered by what others say, what we hear, or by images, tastes, and touches, which can bring us back to where it all started. We may find ourselves rehashing the past, which prevents us from moving forward and enjoying the joy of living. We are encouraged to "remember" the wonders God has performed and His miracles. By refocusing our thoughts on the goodness of God, we prevent the enemy from attacking our minds and causing us to relapse. We need to remember what God has done to stand strong and keep focusing ahead!

Living in a time when emotional intelligence is growing, we are becoming more aware of our feelings and emotions. This heightened understanding equips us to better address emotional wounds and negative thoughts that influence our wellbeing. However, triggers from what others say, what we hear, or sensory experiences can bring us back to painful memories. We might find ourselves stuck, rehashing the past and unable to move forward to fully enjoy life.

We are encouraged to remember the wonders God has performed and His miracles. By refocusing our thoughts on the goodness of God, we prevent the enemy from attacking our minds and causing us to relapse.

Week 3 Tuesday

The Glory and Lifter!

"You, O Lord, are a shield for me, my glory, and the lifter of my head." (Psalm 3:3, AMPC)

When I reflect on this scripture, I am deeply moved by the reminder of our identity in God and His presence in our lives. It's so easy to get weighed down by uncertainty and fear of the unknown. Life often feels like a series of hurdles, and the enemy is quick to amplify our struggles, drawing our focus away from God's promises. Yet, in these moments of doubt, God remains our unfailing beacon of hope.

He is the glory and the lifter of our heads, a steadfast presence in our lives 24/7. No matter how fierce the storms of life may be, God stands as our shield, unwavering and strong. It's crucial to realign our thoughts, to remember that within God's protection, His plans, and His destiny, we find true safety.

Challenges and obstacles will inevitably arise, but we can rest assured that God holds our future. He is our guide through every trial, making a way even when we can't see it. In Him, we are not just shielded but uplifted, given the strength to face whatever comes our way. He is, after all, the glory and the lifter of our heads, reminding us to keep our gaze on Him, secure in His promise of unwavering protection and guidance.

Week 3 Wednesday

Live Your Best!

"Whatever your hand finds to do, do it with all your might."
(Ecclesiastes 9:10, NIV)

I've often heard that I'm too selective about my choices in life, but I genuinely believe that we should strive to live our lives to the fullest. Every day is a gift, and once it's gone, it's lost forever. That's why we should seize each moment, cherishing our time with family and friends and creating meaningful, joyful memories.

Instead of fixating on people's shortcomings, making negative remarks, or judging their actions, why not focus on the positive things they bring into our lives? We often dwell more on how others impact us and what we expect from them, rather than appreciating what they've already given us.

We should aim to live our best lives by showing gratitude to those around us, making them feel valued and cherished. Whatever tasks or responsibilities come our way, let's approach them with our full heart and effort. Bless others, pray for them, uplift and encourage them. By doing so, we not only enrich their lives but also train our minds to see the good in every situation.

Remember, everyone you interact with has the potential to experience a touch of God's love through you. So, let's strive to bring out the best in those we encounter, making each moment count and spreading kindness wherever we go.

Week 3 Thursday

Use What You Know!

"He picked up five smooth stones from a stream and put them into his shepherd's bag. Then, armed only with his shepherd's staff and sling, he started across the valley to fight the Philistine."
(1 Samuel 17:40, NLT)

The story of David and Goliath is one of the most captivating and timeless tales ever told. It's about a young shepherd boy, likely between 16 and 19 years old, who faced a giant with nothing but a sling and a handful of smooth stones. Unlike the soldiers who were fully armed, David had no sword, no armor, no helmet, and no shoes. He stood alone, a mere boy against a seasoned warrior.

David could have easily let fear and intimidation overwhelm him. He could have chosen to back down, just like the king's soldiers who trembled at the sight of Goliath. But David saw beyond the apparent odds. He believed in the power of what he had—his faith and his courage.

We should view ourselves through David's eyes, equipped with exactly what we need to achieve our own destinies. Even if our resources seem limited or unconventional, God provides us with everything necessary to overcome the giants in our lives. Never underestimate the potential within you or the plans God has for you. Embrace the tools and strengths you have, no matter how modest they may seem, and trust that they are exactly what you need to make a significant impact.

Week 3 Friday

Life Up Your Head

"Lift up your heads, you gates; lift them up, you ancient doors, that the King of glory may come in. Who is he, this King of glory? The LORD Almighty—he is the King of glory." (Psalm 24:9–10, NIV)

We're often encouraged to "lift up your head, and the King of glory will come in." It's so easy to let ourselves be bogged down by worries and fears, expecting the worst from every situation we face. But why should we let ourselves be consumed by anxiety? Our thoughts alone won't change anything unless we take action.

When we're reminded to lift up our heads and look around, it's an invitation to open our eyes to the presence of the King of glory. God wants us to witness His power in action, to see how He can transform our struggles and make things right.

We need to train our minds to focus on the light at the end of the tunnel, to nurture hope that things can and will get better. By lifting our heads and keeping our hearts open in prayer, we allow ourselves to experience the profound change that God can bring into our lives. He is the Lord God Almighty, capable of guiding us through our trials and lifting us above our worries. So today, lift up your head, hold fast to hope, and keep reaching out to the King of glory. He is with you, ready to make a way where there seems to be none.

Week 4 Monday

Believe Without Evidence!

"Then Jesus told him, "Because you have seen me, you have believed; blessed are those who have not seen and yet have believed." (John 20:29, NIV)

Thomas had heard the incredible news that Jesus had risen from the dead, but he couldn't bring himself to believe without seeing physical evidence. It's easy to relate to Thomas. Many of us find ourselves seeking tangible proof to believe in God or wanting to see something concrete before we fully trust.

But here's the truth: God is not bound by our need for proof. He doesn't have to show us physical evidence of His existence, nor is He required to mend our brokenness, fix our mistakes, or provide for us. His actions come from His boundless love and grace, not from an obligation to prove Himself.

God assures us that when we choose to believe without needing physical evidence, we are truly blessed. This kind of faith opens doors to healing, provision, and the fulfillment of our deepest needs. It's a testament to His desire for the best in our lives. His love is so profound that He goes above and beyond, caring for us in ways we might not always see but can always trust.

So, even when we can't see the answers or touch the evidence, we can still hold on to the certainty of His love and provision. Trust that His blessings are flowing into your life, guiding and supporting you in every way.

Week 4 Tuesday

Stop, and Praise The Lord!

"Oh, magnify the LORD with me, and let us exalt His name together." (Psalm 34:3, NKJV)

As much as we might dream of living a carefree life, the reality is that it's simply not possible. Navigating relationships with people who have different likes, dislikes, personalities, and opinions can be challenging. We won't always be able to please everyone, and some may take things to heart, adding to our stress.

When we face these challenges and they start to affect our mental well-being, it's crucial to pause and turn our focus to praise. When life feels overwhelming, when the obstacles seem insurmountable, or when you're caught in a whirlwind of negative thoughts, take a moment to stop and praise the Lord.

Praise isn't just a routine; it's a powerful act that brings us closer to God's presence. When we lift up His name and magnify Him, we draw all of heaven to us, and His presence begins to work in our lives. It's in these moments of praise that we find strength, clarity, and peace.

So, no matter how tough things get, keep praising the Lord. Even when you feel tempted or burdened, continue to exalt Him. Your praise opens the door to divine support and shifts your perspective, reminding you that you're never alone. Embrace the power of praise and let it uplift your spirit and guide you through every challenge.

Week 4 Wednesday

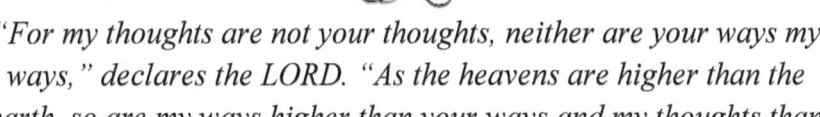
What's God Thinking

"For my thoughts are not your thoughts, neither are your ways my ways," declares the LORD. "As the heavens are higher than the earth, so are my ways higher than your ways and my thoughts than your thoughts." (Isaiah 55:8–9, NIV)

Wow, wow, wow! It's truly uplifting to remind ourselves of this powerful scripture. Have you ever wondered what God's thoughts are about you? I can't imagine Him ever having negative thoughts. Just thinking about it brings such relief and comfort, knowing that no matter what challenges come our way, God always has our best interests at heart and is working to make a way for us.

His thoughts and plans are so much higher than ours. When obstacles seem insurmountable and doors appear to be closing, it's crucial to remember that God's perspective is far greater. He sees beyond our current circumstances and knows the bigger picture.

There's no need to succumb to anger, bitterness, or self-pity. Instead, let's embrace the assurance that God has an incredible plan for our futures—one that surpasses anything we could ever imagine. His plans are filled with hope and promise.

So, remind yourself today that God is thinking about you, always planning a way out of your current situation and guiding you toward a future that's better than you could ever dream. Trust in His divine perspective and keep faith that His plan is unfolding just as it should.

Week 4 Thursday

More Chapters to Live Out!

"There has never been the slightest doubt in my mind that the God who started this great work in you would keep at it and bring it to a flourishing finish on the very day Christ Jesus appears."
(Philippians 1:6, MSG)

God's plan for our lives is to ensure that our stories don't end without achieving the purpose He has designed for us. When we encounter obstacles, setbacks, delays, hurts, and disappointments, it's important to remain encouraged. Think of these challenges as just one chapter in your life's book, with many more chapters waiting to be written.

You have countless experiences ahead, filled with success stories, lives you'll touch, and moments of awe that will reflect signs, wonders, and miracles. This scripture reassures us that the God who started a good work in us is faithful to see it through to completion.

Even when it feels tough, remember to keep pushing forward. The end results are worth it, and there are incredible chapters of your life still to be discovered. In those chapters, you will witness God's hand guiding your path and revealing His plans for you.

So, stay hopeful and trust in the journey. Great things are on the horizon, and each new chapter holds the promise of God's ongoing work in your life. Embrace the journey with faith and anticipation, knowing that each step brings you closer to the fulfillment of your divine purpose.

Week 4 Friday

Focus On The Goodness!

"What would have become of me had I not, believed that I would see the Lord's goodness in the land of the living!"
(Psalm 27:13, AMPC)

As a teenager, David spent his days as a humble shepherd in the fields, tending to his father's sheep. Like many of us, he had grand dreams for his future, but his potential went unnoticed, even by his own family. It would have been easy for David to feel discouraged or to consider giving up on his dreams. Instead, he chose to deepen his relationship with God and strengthen his faith.

David held onto the belief that he would witness God's goodness, even when the odds seemed stacked against him. He nurtured his confidence in God, refusing to let the passage of time or his seemingly insignificant role shake his trust. Then, out of the blue, the prophet Samuel arrived at his home and anointed him to be king—a moment that changed everything for David.

Just like David, we are called to stay focused on the goodness of God, even when we feel overlooked or unrecognized. Trust that there will come a time when God's favor will shine upon you in ways you never expected. God has a way of surprising us and lifting us up, even when we feel insignificant. So hold fast to your faith and confidence, knowing that you, too, will witness the remarkable goodness of God in your life.

Week 5 Monday

His Eyes Is With Us!

"The eyes of the LORD search the whole earth in order to strengthen those whose hearts are fully committed to him." (2 Chronicles 16:9, NLT)

What a powerful scripture this is! It reminds us that the eyes of the Lord are constantly searching the entire earth, ensuring that nothing and no one is overlooked. God's watchful gaze is always on us, guiding and aligning us with the destiny He has prepared for us.

When the enemy attempts to disrupt our lives, God is right there, crafting alternative plans so we are never left feeling stuck. He sees us in our moments of lost hope, when we struggle to recognize our own worth, and when we're under attack. His eyes are always on the lookout for those whose hearts are fully committed to Him, ready to strengthen and uplift them.

The key is to remain wholeheartedly devoted to God. When we are fully committed, His eyes are drawn to us, bringing us the strength and support we need. Even in times when we feel misunderstood or isolated, we can find comfort in knowing that God's eyes are upon us, watching over us with love and care.

So, be encouraged! No matter where you are or how alone you might feel, remember that God's eyes are always on you. His presence is a constant source of strength and reassurance, guiding you through every challenge and blessing you with His unwavering support.

Week 5 Tuesday

He Will Snatch You!

"You saw how I snatched you from the bonds of slavery and carried you on eagles' wings and brought you to Myself."
(Exodus 19:4, VOICE)

What a powerful promise this is! God is committed to delivering us from whatever we feel enslaved by. Whether it's loneliness, depression, anxiety, worry, financial struggles, addictions, or heartaches—anything that weighs us down and makes us feel oppressed or unjustly treated—God promises to lift us out of it and elevate us on eagle's wings.

He will raise us above our difficulties, offering us true freedom and drawing us nearer to Himself. The closer we come to God, the more we experience freedom, peace, joy, and unexpected blessings. His presence brings favor and abundance into our lives in ways we might not have imagined.

So, get ready! God's presence is on its way to rescue you from your challenging circumstances. Picture yourself being lifted up on eagle's wings, soaring above your struggles. As you draw closer to Him, embrace the freedom and peace that come with His embrace. Feel the weight of your burdens lift and the joy of His closeness fill your heart. God is ready to transform your situation and shower you with His incredible blessings.

Your Best Interests At Heart!

"But God made the earth by his power; he founded the world by his wisdom and stretched out the heavens by his understanding."
(Jeremiah 10:12, NIV)

People have always been curious about the origins of the world, coming up with countless theories, beliefs, and opinions. But for us, it's clear that God created everything with His immense power, boundless wisdom, and deep understanding. Just think about the breathtaking beauty of the skies, the intricate design of trees, the soothing flow of waters, and the vibrant life of birds and animals. If God can create all this wonder, imagine what He has in store for you!

God works in ways that often surpass our understanding, delighting and surprising us along the way. Never underestimate what He can do in your life. He has the power to open doors you never thought possible, lead you to places beyond your wildest dreams, and connect you with people you never imagined.

So, don't be surprised by the incredible things God can accomplish. He truly has your best interests at heart, and His plans for you are far greater than you can envision. Embrace the possibility of amazing surprises and opportunities, knowing that God is working in your life with the same creativity and power that shaped the world. Trust in His plans and look forward to the remarkable things He has in store for you!

Week 5 Thursday

Don't Put It Off

"As Paul talked about righteousness, self-control and the judgment to come, Felix was afraid and said, "That's enough for now! You may leave. When I find it convenient, I will send for you."
(Acts 24:25, NIV)

Paul sought to share the gospel with Felix, a Roman governor over Judea. God orchestrated their encounter so Felix could hear about Jesus. However, Felix hesitated and delayed taking action. This was Felix's moment to embrace God's grace, yet he put it off. Often, God speaks to us and brings people into our lives to guide us to the next level, but we miss these pivotal moments. Everyone has valuable insights to offer, and it's crucial to listen and seize the opportunity rather than delay. We can miss out on God's best for our lives when we dismiss people and neglect to make time to listen.

Through prayer and communication with God, He speaks to our hearts and often sends others to confirm His message. It's so important to recognize these divine encounters and not let them pass by unnoticed. Embracing change can be a defining moment in our destiny—don't delay it! Taking action on God's guidance can lead to incredible transformations in our lives. We must be open, attentive, and ready to move when He calls. Remember, God's timing is perfect, and His plans for us are filled with hope and promise. Let's not hesitate when He reaches out to us through others. Embrace the change, and trust that God is leading you to a brighter future.

Week 5 Friday

What Are You Listening To?

"If someone listens to God's word but doesn't do what it says, he is like a person who looks at his face in a mirror, studies his features, goes away, and immediately forgets what he looks like."
(James 1:23–24, GW)

This is a heartfelt reminder of the importance of truly listening to the Word of God and understanding its message for us. It's not enough to just hear; we must also act on it. Otherwise, we are like someone who looks in a mirror, walks away, and forgets their reflection. What is the Word of God saying to you today? For me, it's been clear: God is for me. His goodness and mercy are relentlessly pursuing me. He wants me to thrive and be in good health. He is with me, never against me, working behind the scenes to help fulfill my destiny.

Scripture reminds us, "I can do all things through Christ," which tells us, "Ask, and it shall be given unto you." There are no limits to what we can ask of God. It also says, "If I obey His commands, His blessings will come upon me and my generation." We need to embrace and hold onto God's Word as firmly as we remember our reflection in the mirror.

Sometimes, we might not like what we see in the mirror. But remember, our past, others' opinions, and our mistakes don't define us. God defines who we are, and He sees us as blessed and highly favored. Trust in His vision of you, and let His Word shape your life.

Week 6 Monday

Self-Care Deposits!

"If you faint in the day of adversity, your strength is small."
(Proverbs 24:10, NKJV)

Every day, it feels like we're all giving a piece of ourselves to the world—whether through our jobs, our roles as parents, our relationships, or our friendships. It's a rhythm we've grown accustomed to, where we continually offer our time, energy, and love. But think about it like a bank account: if we keep making withdrawals without ever making a deposit, eventually the account runs dry. The same goes for us. If we don't make space for self-care, if we don't pause to replenish our emotional, physical, mental, and spiritual reserves, we risk running on empty.

Imagine if you never refilled your energy or took moments to recharge; it would be hard to keep up with the demands of daily life. Even Jesus recognized this need for renewal and often stepped away from the crowds to find solitude and refresh. It's a powerful reminder that to thrive in every facet of life, we must first nurture ourselves.

So, take a moment—make it a priority—to invest in self-care. Treat it as a crucial deposit in your well-being account. By doing so, you'll find that you're not only better equipped to handle life's challenges but also more able to bring your best to everything you do. Self-care isn't just a luxury; it's a necessity for sustaining the energy and enthusiasm you bring to the world.

Week 6 Tuesday

Factual or Fictional?

"Be careful what you think, because your thoughts run your life." Proverbs 4:23, NCV

The scriptures offer profound wisdom for navigating our daily lives. Did you know we have about 70,000 thoughts a day, many of which are more about friction than fact? It's easy to let these thoughts spiral into disappointment, fear, or anxiety, shaping our lives in ways that pull us down rather than lift us up. That's why it's so important to focus on thinking positively.

Dreaming is more than just imagining; it's about setting goals and turning those dreams into reality. From a young age, we've learned to dream without limits, and those dreams have a profound impact on who we are today. But our thoughts can easily sway us towards negativity if we let them. When our minds dwell on thoughts that don't serve us, it's time to hit reset and replace them with thoughts that align with positivity and possibility.

Think of it this way: when we dream big and align our desires with God's will, we open ourselves up to His guidance and blessings. God wants to fulfill the desires of our hearts, but for that to happen, our thoughts must reflect His truth and love. By focusing on what's factual and letting go of the fictional, we allow ourselves to be led by divine wisdom and live a life full of purpose and hope.

Week 6 Wednesday

Expect The Unexpected!

"Then Peter said, "Silver or gold I do not have, but what I do have I give you. In the name of Jesus Christ of Nazareth, walk."
(Acts 3:6, NIV)

Imagine a man who had been crippled since birth, spending his days begging for alms at the temple gate—a place where many sought help. This man might have even seen Jesus during His time on earth, but his situation remained unchanged. One day, as Peter and John passed by, the man reached out, hoping for a coin to sustain him. Instead of silver or gold, Peter offered something far greater. He said, "Silver or gold I do not have, but what I do have I give you. In the name of Jesus Christ of Nazareth, walk."

To the man's astonishment, he found the strength to stand, and joyously began dancing and praising God. His moment of transformation was not just a miracle—it was a testament to faith and expectation. Some of us have been waiting and hoping for our own miracles, just like this man.

We, too, need to stretch out our hands with the same expectation. God calls us to be proactive, to ask with faith and to anticipate His blessings. He might work through others, just as He did through Peter, or He might surprise us in unexpected ways. Embrace the possibility of the miraculous and trust that God's timing is perfect. Dance with joy and praise Him, knowing that miracles are often just around the corner.

Week 6 Thursday

The Power In Meditating

"Keep this Book of the Law always on your lips; meditate on it day and night, so that you may be careful to do everything written in it. Then you will be prosperous and successful." (Joshua 1:8, NIV)

Imagine having a state-of-the-art gadget but not knowing how to use it—its incredible potential goes untapped. This is similar to how a lack of knowledge can limit our experience of life's fullness. Many of us miss out on the richness of life simply because we don't understand what we're entitled to or how things work. That's why we're encouraged to immerse ourselves in the Word. The scripture tells us, "Keep this Book of the Law always on your lips; meditate on it day and night, so that you may be careful to do everything written in it. Then you will be prosperous and successful."

Meditation here isn't just about casual thinking; it's about deeply focusing on and repeating the promises of God until they become a part of us. This process of reflection and repetition is meant to help us live out those promises, leading us to prosperity and success. Yet, the enemy knows the power that comes from this practice and distracts us with past regrets, fears, and endless distractions. We often find ourselves reading everything but the Bible—news, emails, books, you name it—while the Word remains untouched.

Choosing to read and meditate on the Bible is a conscious decision to unlock its transformative power. By making time for the Word, we tap into its life-changing potential and align ourselves with God's promises. Let's embrace this opportunity to enrich our lives and experience the fullness that God intends for us.

Week 6 Friday

I Will Arise!!!

"I will arise and go to my father, and will say to him, 'Father, I have sinned against heaven and before you.'" (Luke 15:18, NKJV)

The story of the prodigal son is a powerful reminder of redemption and transformation. After squandering his inheritance and hitting rock bottom, the young man found himself with nothing—feeding pigs and even eating their slop. It was in this moment of utter despair that he had a revelation. He remembered the comfort and abundance he once had and realized it was time for a change.

He decided, "I will arise." This decision marked the first step toward reclaiming his life. The second step was returning to his source of support—his home, a place where he was loved and accepted, where his journey had begun. It was a sanctuary of refuge and hope. Finally, he sought reconciliation, finding peace with himself and with his father.

This story speaks to all of us. No matter where we find ourselves in life, we can follow the same path to renewal. We need to rise above our circumstances, return to our source of strength and comfort, which is God, and make peace with ourselves and anyone we may have hurt. By doing this, we open ourselves to blessings and restoration. Our Father's love is boundless, and He will always welcome us back with open arms.

Week 7 Monday

He Will Rescue

"Do not be afraid of them, for I am with you and will rescue you," declares the LORD." (Jeremiah 1:8, NIV)

God had a powerful plan for Jeremiah, telling him that before he was even born, He had set him apart to be a prophet to the nations. Despite this divine calling, Jeremiah was overwhelmed with fear and felt unqualified for such a significant role. But God spoke directly to his heart, reassuring him that He was with him and urging him not to be afraid. He promised that He would rescue Jeremiah from any challenges he faced.

This promise is not just for Jeremiah; it's for each of us. The same God who stood by Jeremiah is with us today. He is our refuge and strength, and we need not be consumed by fear. Fear often brings anxiety and stress, clouding our minds and making it difficult to function. It can create insecurities that hold us back from reaching our true potential.

We must remember that God is by our side, just as He was with Jeremiah. Instead of allowing fear to dictate our lives, we should embrace courage and trust in God's presence. By doing so, we can overcome our insecurities and step into the destiny He has designed for us. Let's hold on to the assurance that God's strength is with us, empowering us to face our fears and live fully.

Week 7 Tuesday

We Are No Surprise to God!

"Before I formed you in the womb I knew you, before you were born I set you apart; I appointed you as a prophet to the nations." (Jeremiah 1:5, NIV)

No pregnancy takes God by surprise, nor does any birth. From the moment of conception, God already has a plan in place for each of us. While sin and its consequences bring death, sickness, and suffering into our lives, we must remember that although we might be unexpected to our parents, we are never unexpected to God.

It's easy to feel disheartened when things don't go as planned and to question why life seems so challenging. However, we must recognize that there's a spiritual battle at play. God has a beautiful plan and a hopeful future for us, but the enemy seeks to bring destruction and turmoil. Just as God spoke favor and blessings over Jeremiah, He has done the same for us. We have been given purpose, status, and a special place in His heart.

God will fight for us against every negative force that tries to pull us down. Though He grants us the freedom to make choices, He never abandons us when we falter. His power is always at work to guide us back to the right path. Embrace the destiny God has set before you and trust Him to lead you with His wisdom and love. Remember, your future is bright with Him guiding your steps!

Week 7 Wednesday

Live With Compassion

"While he was still a long way off, his father saw him and was filled with compassion for him; he ran to his son, threw his arms around him and kissed him." (Luke 15:20, NIV)

The story of the prodigal son really touches my heart. It beautifully illustrates God's endless compassion, as represented by the father in this story. Despite his son's departure and the mistakes he made, the father's love never wavered. Scripture tells us that while the son was still a long way off, his father saw him, and his heart was immediately filled with compassion. He didn't walk but ran to his son, embracing him with open arms and kissing him, even though the son was dirty and smelled of the pigsty.

Imagine the scene: the son, covered in grime and rags, was met not with judgment, but with a flood of unconditional love. This kind of compassion sees beyond the surface, recognizing the opportunity to show love and hope for transformation. When we live with such compassion, it reshapes our perspective on life. Our hearts become tuned to value and worth, rather than flaws and mistakes.

Living with compassion means approaching life with kindness and care. It's about nurturing a mindset that mirrors God's love. Whether with a spouse, children, friends, or even those who have hurt us, we have countless chances to express this unconditional love. Let's seize every opportunity to show compassion and reflect God's incredible grace in our interactions.

Week 7 Thursday

No Weapon

"No weapon formed against you shall prosper, And every tongue which rises against you in judgment You shall condemn. This is the heritage of the servants of the Lord..." (Isaiah 54:17, NKJV)

When we think of weapons, our minds might immediately go to swords, knives, or guns—things designed to inflict harm. Yet, words can wield a similar destructive power, deeply affecting our emotional well-being. Life's unexpected challenges can also feel like weapons, causing wounds that touch us physically, mentally, spiritually, and psychologically.

But there's a powerful truth we can hold onto: no weapon formed against us has the power to truly defeat us. Whether it's sickness, financial difficulties, unemployment, or the weight of past hurts and regrets, none of these challenges can claim victory over us. The scripture reassures us, "No weapon formed against you shall prosper." Whatever tries to bring us down will not succeed. Moreover, the scripture tells us that "every tongue which rises against you in judgment You shall condemn." God promises to counteract any negative words spoken against us, rendering them powerless. This is our heritage as the servants of the Lord—a promise of protection and victory.

Align yourself with where God wants you to be, embracing the strength and assurance He provides. Even in the face of adversity, you are upheld by divine promise and protection. Let this truth anchor you, knowing that no weapon or word can truly harm you when you are aligned with God's purpose for your life.

Week 7 Friday

Boast about Him!

"But let him who boasts boast in this, that he understands and knows me, that I am the LORD who practices steadfast love, justice, and righteousness in the earth." (Jeremiah 9:24, ESV)

To truly boast about someone, you need to genuinely know and understand them. When we boast about the Lord, it comes from a deep place of pride and appreciation for who He is and what He has done in our lives. It means recognizing that He has taken care of us, protecting us from our enemies and guiding us through every trial. His love for us is so profound that we remain steadfast, regardless of the negativity or doubts others may throw our way.

Knowing God means having unwavering confidence in His strength and supremacy. He is greater and more powerful than anything or anyone we could face. As the Creator of the universe, He has consistently proven His faithfulness to humanity throughout history.

Today, let's celebrate and boast about the goodness of God with full confidence. Remember that He is our God—our protector, our guide, and our source of unwavering strength. Share His greatness with others, not just as an abstract concept, but as a personal testimony of how He has touched and transformed your life. Embrace the joy of knowing Him deeply and let that knowledge fuel your praise and thanksgiving.

Week 8 Monday

You Are Qualified!

"Go with the strength you have, and rescue Israel from the Midianites. I am sending you!" (Judges 6:14, NLT)

Imagine God speaking directly to you, saying, "Go with the strength you have; I am sending you!" How would you respond? This is exactly what happened to Gideon. At the time, he was hiding from the enemy, overwhelmed by fear and uncertainty. Yet, an angel appeared and told him that he was chosen to lead the Israelites into battle, calling him a mighty man of courage.

Gideon was at a pivotal moment in his life. Deep down, he sensed God's calling but struggled with feelings of inadequacy. He didn't see himself as qualified, and his mind was likely swamped with fears, anxieties, and insecurities. It's a place many of us find ourselves in—facing challenges that seem insurmountable and running from what we view as our adversaries.

But God's message is clear: even when we feel unprepared or inadequate, He sees us as qualified and equipped for the task at hand. God doesn't measure our strength by our own standards but by His power working through us. Nothing can obstruct your destiny except your own self-doubt. So, embrace the strength you have, knowing it's enough to confront and overcome your challenges. Don't give up or disqualify yourself. Step forward with faith, for God is with you every step of the way.

Week 8 Tuesday
Your Joy Is Your Strength!

"No one can take your joy from you." (John 16:22, NLV)

Joy is a precious gem, a divine gift placed within each of us by God. It's something that resides deep in our hearts, no matter the circumstances. Even when faced with belligerent, rude, or avoidant people, it's crucial not to let their behavior dim the light of your joy. Their actions might be intended to make you feel insignificant, but don't let that impact your inner happiness.

When someone tries to undermine your sense of worth, remember that their opinion doesn't define you. You are not bound by their negativity or judgment. You possess greatness within you and have no reason to lower yourself to their level. Instead, rise above and keep moving forward with confidence.

The enemy will often target your joy, trying to cast shadows of sadness, anxiety, and loneliness. He knows that joy is your strength, and by attacking it, he aims to weaken you. So, stand firm and protect your joy. When you feel the weight of negativity, counter it by playing some uplifting music, singing, and dancing. Let the joy within you burst forth and energize your spirit. Embrace your joy as the powerful force it is, and let it be the light that guides you through every challenge.

Week 8 Wednesday

God Has The Final Say

"The suffering won't last forever. It won't be long before this generous God who has great plans for us in Christ—eternal and glorious plans they are!—will have you put together and on your feet for good. He gets the last word; yes, he does. "
(1 Peter 5:10–11, MSG)

We all go through different seasons in life, and sometimes, those seasons feel like intense suffering. I've been there, feeling trapped in a dark hole of hopelessness, believing that God wasn't listening or making a way. These difficult times can stem from issues with health, finances, marriage, relationships, or employment. But as the scripture reassures us, "The suffering won't last forever." It's just a season, and we must hold on to our faith, reminding ourselves that God is working behind the scenes to bring about a solution.

The scripture also tells us, "It won't be long before this generous God, who has great plans for us in Christ..." Our God is generous in His solutions and indeed has a plan for each of us. He "will have you put together and on your feet for good." God promises to bring things together and restore us to a place of stability. We might feel down and out for a while, but it won't last forever. Remember, "He gets the last word; yes, he does." Regardless of what we see happening around us, our God has the final say.

Hold on to this truth. Even in the darkest seasons, know that they are temporary. God's plan for you is one of restoration and hope, and He is always at work, even when we can't see it. Trust in His timing and remain steadfast in your faith.

Week 8 Thursday

With Open Arms!

" "The father said, 'Quick, bring me the best robe, my very own robe, and I will place it on his shoulders. Bring the ring, the seal of sonship, and I will put it on his finger. And bring out the best shoes you can find for my son.' " (Luke 15:22, TPT)

We've all stumbled and made mistakes. None of us are perfect, and the weight of regret can sometimes feel overwhelming. Impulsive decisions driven by emotions can strain or even sever relationships with those we love. However, scripture teaches us that when we humble ourselves and seek to make amends, restoration is possible.

God's grace is boundless. When we turn back to Him and admit our wrongs, He welcomes us with open arms, ready to restore our joy, gifts, favors, and blessings. This restoration isn't just a partial repair but a complete renewal. It's important to release negative thoughts about our past mistakes. The enemy thrives on our guilt and uses it to keep us from embracing God's forgiveness and grace.

Instead, we should fill our minds with God's thoughts and promises. Remember, He will never give up on us, no matter how far we've strayed or how many mistakes we've made. By aligning our thinking with His, we can overcome the enemy's attempts to use our past against us.

So, let's embrace humility, seek restoration, and remember that God's love and mercy are always available to us. He is always ready to lift us up and bring us back into His favor. Keep moving forward, knowing that you are never beyond His reach and that His plans for you are full of hope and renewal.

Week 8 Friday

No Need To Hide!

"Then the man and his wife heard the sound of the LORD God as he was walking in the garden in the cool of the day, and they hid from the LORD God among the trees of the garden. But the LORD God called to the man, "Where are you?" (Genesis 3:8–9, NIV)

Adam and Eve once enjoyed a beautiful connection with God in the Garden of Eden. Genesis paints a picture of them basking in God's love, feeling secure and joyful in His presence. However, their disobedience shattered this harmony, bringing in feelings of condemnation and fear. Aware of their wrongdoing, they hid from God. Yet, even in their estrangement, God called out to them, asking, "Adam, where are you?"

Despite our own failings, when we come into God's presence, we have nothing to hide. We can be confident in His love for us. Regardless of our mistakes and flaws, He accepts us just as we are. There is no need to hide or feel condemned.

Return to His presence, where acceptance and love await. In God's presence, we find the security and joy that Adam and Eve once knew. We are reminded that, despite our imperfections, God's love remains steadfast. It's a place where we can be our true selves, free from fear and shame. Embrace the confidence that comes from knowing you are loved and accepted by Him. Let go of the need to hide and step boldly into the warmth of His embrace.

Week 9 Monday
Only To Become Better

"See, I have refined you, though not as silver; I have tested you in the furnace of affliction." (Isaiah 48:10, NIV)

When I think of refining, it reminds me of the nurturing process parents provide for their children. It's natural for us to want to remove anything negative or unwanted from their lives, always striving to make things better. Refinement is about constant improvement and growth. When life presents challenges, we should view them as opportunities to become stronger and wiser.

Our faith grows as we gain wisdom through the refining of our experiences. Despite facing some major stressors in my life, I've come to realize that God isn't focused on changing my circumstances, but on changing me. This perspective shift has been transformative, helping me see challenges as part of God's plan to shape me into a better version of myself.

So, embrace God's refining work in your life. Trust that each hardship and trial is a tool in His hands, crafting you into who you're meant to be. It's not always easy, but remember that this process is driven by His love and desire for your growth. Allow His work to mold you, knowing that the end result is a more resilient, wiser, and stronger you. Celebrate the journey of refinement, and take heart in knowing that God is with you every step of the way, guiding you toward your best self.

Week 9 Tuesday

The Eyes Our Guiding Light

"The eye is the lamp of the body. So if your eye is sound, your entire body will be full of light. But if your eye is unsound, your whole body will be full of darkness. If then the very light in you [your conscience] is darkened, how dense is that darkness!"
(Matthew 6:22–23, AMPC)

Scripture speaks to the very essence of our being, reminding us that our spiritual eyes are the guiding light of our conscience. This inner beacon illuminates our path, shaping our thoughts and actions. What we allow our eyes to see is crucial, as it influences the light within us. Some sights can cast shadows, leaving scars on our souls from traumas, abuses, wrong choices, and mistakes, chaining us to darkness. Even engaging in actions we know are wrong leads us down negative paths.

We must listen to the gentle whispers of our conscience, guarding our eyes against toxic influences. When we protect our spiritual vision, we nurture a clear conscience, lifting the heavy burden of condemnation. This clarity fills our lives with boundless joy and peace. Imagine the freedom of living without the weight of past mistakes and wrongdoings. It starts with what we allow into our minds and hearts through our eyes. By choosing to focus on the light of God, we let His love and wisdom shine within us, guiding us toward a life of fulfillment and purpose.

Embrace this guiding light, and let it illuminate your mind and soul. Trust in the power of a clear conscience to bring you joy and serenity. Let your eyes reflect the light of God, leading you on a path of righteousness and peace.

Week 9 Wednesday

Gifted with Treasures!

"Creation itself is on tiptoe with expectation, eagerly awaiting the moment when God's children will be revealed."
(Romans 8:19, NTE)

Yesterday, we went out for dinner with one of our daughters, her husband, and their two children. As we sat eating, I noticed some rings on her finger. Curious, I discovered they were made from spoons—bent, polished, and shining, they looked beautiful and expensive. My daughter has been making these rings as a hobby, and in that moment, I realized the greatness within us all. We are filled with creativity and talents, gifted to us by God.

Often, we focus too much on the challenges and attacks that come our way, forgetting the treasures God has deposited within us. It's essential to remember who we are and the bright, blessed destiny God has planned for us. It's easy to be distracted and overlook the potential inside us, but we must remind ourselves that there's so much waiting to be discovered.

Let's tap into the treasures God has placed within us. The scripture beautifully says, "Creation itself is on tiptoe with expectation, eagerly awaiting the moment when God's children will be revealed." This is a powerful reminder that the world is waiting for us to uncover and share our God-given gifts.

So, let's embrace our creativity and talents, knowing that they are part of God's plan for our lives. By doing so, we not only honor Him but also enrich our lives and the lives of those around us.

Week 9 Thursday

God Believes In You!

"And we know that God causes everything to work together for the good of those who love God and are called according to his purpose for them." (Romans 8:28, NLT)

Who could imagine that greater works are possible when Jesus already accomplished the greatest work known to man? During His time on earth, Jesus performed extraordinary miracles. He healed the sick, gave sight to the blind, and even raised the dead. Multitudes followed Him, captivated by His wisdom, compassion, and authority. His teachings weren't just profound—they transformed lives. Yet, this same Jesus, now living within us, declared, *"Whoever believes in me will also do the works that I do; and greater works than these will he do, because I am going to the Father."*

This powerful truth challenges us to embrace the incredible potential God has placed within us. It takes faith to believe that the Creator of the universe desires to work through us to continue His mission. The "greater works" Jesus referred to are not about surpassing Him in power or significance but about extending His reach through the Spirit. What Jesus began in His earthly ministry, we are now called to carry forward in a world longing for hope and healing.

When we step out in faith, we become conduits for God's love, grace, and power. Through prayer, acts of kindness, encouragement, and service, we can touch the lives of those around us. God doesn't ask us to be extraordinary; He asks us to be willing. Our role is to trust Him, take bold steps, and allow Him to work through us.

Imagine what God can do through a heart fully surrendered to Him! You are a vessel uniquely positioned to demonstrate His goodness.

Week 9 Friday

Willing and Ready

"Oh, how great is your goodness to those who publicly declare that you will rescue them. For you have stored up great blessings for those who trust and reverence you." (Psalm 31:19, TLB)

We all encounter obstacles from time to time, and often, they come without warning. These unexpected situations stretch us, challenging our ability to trust in God. It's relatively easy to trust Him when we can see potential solutions on the horizon—this is a measure of faith. But what happens when the situation feels utterly hopeless? In those moments, it's common to feel overwhelmed, descending into a state of panic or fear. Yet, this is where greater faith is required—the kind of faith that believes in God's power even when the odds seem insurmountable.

Consider the story of the disciples in the storm. As the winds raged and the waves crashed, fear gripped their hearts. In their distress, Jesus addressed them, saying, *"Why are you afraid, O you of little faith?"* His words serve as a reminder for us today. Like the disciples, we may feel caught in a storm, surrounded by chaos. But Jesus doesn't leave us to face the storm alone.

The scripture recounts how Jesus took action: *"Then He rose and rebuked the winds and the sea, and there was a great calm."* This powerful moment illustrates not only His authority over the elements but also His deep care for His people.

Jesus is the same yesterday, today, and forever. Just as He calmed the storm for the disciples, He is willing and able to bring peace to your life. No matter how turbulent your situation may seem, you can reach out to Him.

Week 10 Monday

Don't Stop Growing

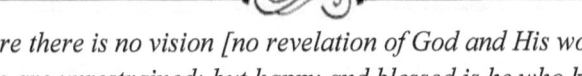

"Where there is no vision [no revelation of God and His word], the people are unrestrained; but happy and blessed is he who keeps the law [of God]." (Proverbs 29:18, AMP)

What a powerful and encouraging promise this is! The righteous are likened to palm trees—trees that remain steadfast through storms. Despite fierce winds, palm trees don't break; instead, their roots grow deeper, securing their foundation. Similarly, the majestic cedars of Lebanon are known for their strength, longevity, and resilience. These comparisons remind us that no matter what life throws our way, God has equipped us to grow and thrive through every season.

We must resist the temptation to let life's challenges halt our progress. Hardship is not the end of growth; it's an opportunity to deepen our roots in God's Word and presence. As long as we are "planted in the house of the LORD," we will flourish. This flourishing is not bound by age or circumstances. God promises that we will still bear fruit, even in old age.

There is no limit to how God can use us. We can volunteer, encourage others, learn new skills, or share wisdom. Every day is an opportunity to produce something meaningful and reflect God's glory.

So, don't stop! Keep moving forward, stay rooted in faith, and trust God's promise of growth and fruitfulness. Your life can continue to flourish as you remain grounded in Him. Let's keep growing, no matter the season.

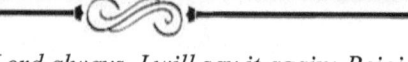

Life Of Joy

Rejoice in the Lord always. I will say it again: Rejoice!"
(Philippians 4:4, NIV)

Life can often leave us feeling overwhelmed—stress, exhaustion, worry, and burnout creeping into our days. But this is not the life God envisioned for us. His plan is for us to live with joy, a joy that is unwavering and not dictated by our circumstances. Joy is a choice we must make, an intentional act of the will, born from within and rooted in faith.

The past, with all its trials and regrets, is beyond our control. So why allow it to rob us of the joy we can experience today? Instead of dwelling on what cannot be changed, we should focus on nurturing a mindset of joy—one that seeks gratitude and finds beauty even in life's challenges. The Bible encourages us, saying, "Rejoice in the Lord always." This command isn't conditional; it applies in every situation. And to underscore its importance, Scripture repeats, "I will say it again: Rejoice!" This repetition serves as a gentle yet firm reminder of the necessity of joy in our lives.

Choosing joy is an act of faith and trust in God's greater plan. It allows us to rise above our circumstances and find peace in His presence. Today, make the choice to embrace joy. Let it light up your heart, touch those around you, and reflect the life of abundance and love that God desires for you. Purpose in your heart to rejoice, and let joy be your guiding light, no matter what lies ahead.

Week 10 Wednesday

Another Touch

"Then Jesus placed his hands on the man's eyes again, and his eyes were opened. His sight was completely restored, and he could see everything clearly." (Mark 8:25, NLT)

When Jesus laid His hands on the blind man, a miracle began to unfold. At first, the man's vision was blurry, his sight unfocused. But with a second touch from Jesus, everything became clear, and he was completely healed. This powerful moment reminds us that transformation is always possible through Him. Many of us carry feelings of inadequacy or discouragement, weighed down by criticism or a lack of confidence. These moments can leave us feeling stuck, uncertain of our path forward.

But just like the blind man, we can experience the life-changing power of Jesus. With just one more touch, our lives can be transformed in ways we never imagined. He is always there, waiting for us to reach out to Him in faith. His love and grace are endless, and He desires to heal not only our struggles but also our hearts.

It's important not to let the words of others or our own self-doubt define who we are. We are children of God, loved and cherished beyond measure. With His touch, burdens can be lifted, hope restored, and clarity found. One encounter with Jesus is enough to change the trajectory of our lives forever.

Let this story of healing inspire you to reach out to Him today. Trust in His power to bring transformation, and remember that His touch is never far away. Just one more touch from Jesus can open the door to a life of renewed purpose and unshakable joy.

Week 10 Thursday

He Gives Rest

"It's useless to rise early and go to bed late, and work your worried fingers to the bone. Don't you know he enjoys giving rest to those he loves?"
(Psalm 127:2, MSG)

In today's fast-paced world, it's easy to find ourselves glued to social media, gaming, texting, and countless other distractions that are just a tap away from morning until night. We hold ourselves and those around us to high expectations of communication, yet often lose sight of what matters most—the meaningful connections that truly nourish our souls. I've heard loved ones share feelings of loneliness, even while surrounded by the people they care about. It's a reminder of how essential it is to find balance in our lives and to be fully present with our families, friends, and colleagues.

We need to resist the urge to rely on our phones for constant stimulation, avoiding that unsettling sense of panic when they're not within reach. Instead, we should take intentional steps to find rest and embrace peace. God, in His goodness, takes joy in providing us with the calm and equilibrium we so deeply need. It's in those moments of stillness that we can reconnect—with ourselves, with Him, and with the people we treasure.

Pause for a moment today. Let go of the endless distractions and appreciate the freedom of simply being present. Set your phone aside, look into the faces of those you love, and enjoy the richness of true connection. In these quiet moments, you'll rediscover the peace and joy that come from focusing on what truly matters most.

Week 10 Friday

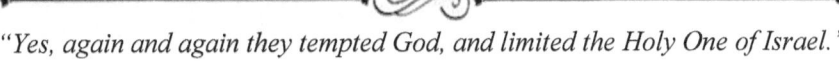
No Limits

"Yes, again and again they tempted God, and limited the Holy One of Israel."
(Psalm 78:41, NKJV)

God promised the Israelites the gift of the Promised Land, yet their journey through the wilderness was anything but easy. They faced numerous challenges, setbacks, and delays. In the midst of their struggles, they began to lose sight of the incredible miracle of their deliverance from slavery, and their hearts filled with complaints. Their story is a reflection of our own. Once enslaved by sin, we too have been set free by God's grace and are on a journey—a journey toward eternity with Him.

It's important to remember that God's power has no limits. His provision is boundless, and He invites us to come to Him without hesitation, asking freely and boldly. We must not let our fears, doubts, or perceived limitations hold us back. Instead, we can place our trust in God, knowing He is faithful to guide us.

God's purpose for calling us is unshakable, and His presence in our lives is steadfast. He will not abandon us. Even in the face of opposition or uncertainty, we can trust Him to provide for our every need, to open doors we never imagined, and to strengthen us for the road ahead.

Today, let's let go of our worries and focus on God's infinite wisdom and love. He will carry us through our wilderness, just as He did for the Israelites, and lead us into the fullness of His promises. Trust in Him, and let His guidance sustain you.

Week 11 Monday

His Favours

"His favor lasts a lifetime." (Psalm 30:5, NIV)

God promises to give us His favour that endures for a lifetime. One thing I've come to cherish deeply is the unwavering love of my parents. As the years pass, their love only grows stronger, and the pride they feel for me is undeniable. It's a love that sets me apart, a reflection of the heart of a parent. But how much greater is the love of our Heavenly Father? His love and favor surpass anything we can imagine.

God's favour isn't confined to moments of ease and comfort. It shines even brighter in our challenges, setbacks, and struggles. When life feels overwhelming, His favour carries us, providing exactly what we need at just the right time. If we paused to reflect on the blessings in our lives, we'd find endless stories of God's provision—encounters with the right people, unexpected opportunities, promotions, new relationships, loans approved against all odds, discounted prices, and countless moments of joy.

These blessings are not fleeting; they are lifelong gifts from a God who delights in surprising us, even in the most unexpected ways. Each day is filled with the potential for His favor to unfold anew.

Take heart, knowing that His favor has no expiration date. Trust in His promises, and embrace the assurance that God's favour is always working, and surrounding you with His boundless love. His blessings are yours to cherish, today and always.

Week 11 Tuesday

Shape Your Thoughts

"Who of you by worrying can add a single hour to your life?"
(Luke 12:25, NIV)

Our thoughts, desires, and aspirations are powerful—they shape the course of our lives, bringing either blessings or challenges. By focusing on the goodness of God and the incredible blessings He has prepared for us and those around us, we can cultivate a life filled with joy and gratitude. Choosing to dwell on His favor and positivity allows us to experience the fullness of His love and provision. Conversely, giving in to negativity and letting worries overwhelm us can hinder our path and rob us of peace.

God's favor surrounds us in every season, bringing opportunities and encounters we could never arrange on our own. Picture His blessings flowing into your life—opportunities unfolding, new doors opening, and connections being made with people who inspire and guide you. Think of good health, abundance, and increase coming your way. Envision His hand directing your steps and preparing a way forward, even in uncertain times. This is the language of God—a language of hope, faith, and boundless possibilities.

Let your mind work in harmony with God's thoughts. When you align your thinking with His promises, you unlock a mindset of peace and joy. Take every opportunity to reflect on His goodness and the abundant plans He has for you. Today, choose to focus on the blessings and favor God has in store, and watch how your life transforms as you embrace His guidance. Let His thoughts fill your mind and His joy fill your heart.

Week 11 Wednesday

He Heals The Cause

"For I will restore health to you and heal you of your wounds," says the LORD." Jeremiah 30:17, NKJV

Reading this scripture brings a fresh perspective. While healing is often associated with physical ailments, the passage speaks to a profound and all-encompassing restoration—healing that reaches deep into the heart and soul. It reminds us that God's power extends far beyond what we can see or touch. Emotional wounds, such as those that lead to mental health struggles like depression and anxiety, are not beyond His reach. Many of the battles we face, including addiction, are rooted in unresolved pain, yet God's promise of healing is for every wound—physical, emotional, and spiritual.

When we turn to God in prayer, we can focus not only on the symptoms of our struggles but on their root causes. By doing so, we invite His transformative and holistic healing into every area of our lives. God's power is limitless, and His desire to heal is driven by His deep love for us. The scripture serves as a beautiful assurance that He is ready and able to restore us fully.

As we open our hearts to His healing, we can trust that He not only addresses the surface but transforms us from within. God's healing isn't just momentary—it's life-changing. Let this encourage you to bring your deepest wounds to Him in faith and trust, knowing that healing begins where His love meets your need. God heals the cause, bringing renewal and restoration. Truly, God is able!

Week 11 Thursday

Be Conformed to The Image

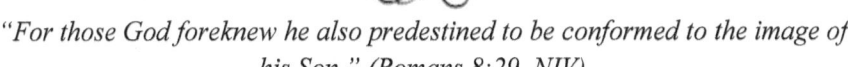

"For those God foreknew he also predestined to be conformed to the image of his Son." (Romans 8:29, NIV)

In the chaos of life, with endless demands pressing upon us, it's natural to feel the weight of stress. Whether it's work, studies, family, or relationships, the pressures can sometimes seem insurmountable. Yet, in the midst of it all, we must hold fast to our true identity as seen through the eyes of God. We were created to reflect His Son, carrying within us His strength, confidence, and assurance. As heirs to a divine legacy, we are destined for freedom and boundless possibilities. Let us align ourselves with His image—the image of victory and purpose.

Life's challenges and obstacles may attempt to block our path, but they are no match for our Heavenly Father, who reigns over all. He holds the power to move mountains, and His vision for our lives is unwavering. Even as difficulties arise, we can trust that He is already crafting a way forward, equipping us with the tools we need to prevail.

When we conform to the image God intended for us, we become a reflection of His glory—a powerful declaration in the spiritual realm. His image speaks triumph, hope, and limitless potential. Take a moment to envision yourself transformed into the person you were created to be. Trust in God's promises, for He is faithful. Let His strength sustain you and His love guide you, knowing that in Him, every challenge is an opportunity for victory. You are destined to walk boldly in His purpose and grace.

Week 11 Friday

Raising Seven!

"And the smoke and fragrant aroma of the incense, with the prayers of the saints (God's people), ascended before God from the angel's hand."
(Revelation 8:4, AMP)

Raising a family of seven children was a journey I could only navigate with God at the center—the solid foundation upon which everything was built. From the moment we woke each morning, our day began with praise and worship, and as night fell, the soothing sound of the Bible being played filled our home. Our devotion emitted a fragrant aroma that invited God's presence into our lives, bringing peace to our home and guiding each of us toward our unique destinies.

Together, we prayed, thanked God for His goodness, and praised Him for His endless blessings. We discussed His faithfulness, reflecting on how He sustained us through challenges and celebrated our victories. As we declared His truths, we believed the angels carried our praises as an offering before God, allowing His presence to dwell among us.

I've seen firsthand how worship transforms lives, attracting God's favor and leading my children toward success in education, fulfilling careers, and meaningful relationships. Witnessing this has strengthened my conviction in the power of praise and worship. God's presence isn't just a fleeting feeling—it's life-changing.

Today, I encourage you to lift your heart in praise and worship to the Lord. Let it be an expression of gratitude and trust, drawing His attention and bringing His peace into your home. Let His guidance and blessings flow abundantly as you honor Him with your worship, just as He intended. The aroma of praise invites miracles.

Week 12 Monday

Love Keeps No Record

"Love...keeps no record of being wronged." (1 Corinthians 13:4–5, NLT)

Forgiveness can be one of life's greatest challenges, especially when it means letting go of the past. Many people find it hard to release the pain caused by others—a friend, family member, or spouse who may have wronged them. They carry a mental list of every mistake, regret, and hurt, unable to move beyond them. Yet, holding onto these burdens only keeps us stuck. To step into a new level of peace and freedom, we must release the past and embrace the present as we journey toward a brighter future.

The Bible reminds us, "Love... keeps no record of being wronged." This powerful truth encourages us to let go of bitterness and resentment. The past, shaped by moments of immaturity, missteps, or decisions made with limited knowledge, cannot be undone. But it also doesn't have to define us. By forgiving and releasing what has been, we free ourselves to focus on the positive choices that lie ahead.

Forgiveness is not about condoning the wrong but about unburdening ourselves and allowing love to lead. When we let go of the pain we've carried for too long, we open our hearts to healing and renewal. Take a step today to forgive—not only others but also yourself. Trust that through forgiveness, you're not only honoring love's true nature but also reclaiming your joy and stepping into the future God has in store for you.

Week 12 Tuesday

Ask Specific!

"Jabez prayed to the God of Israel: "Bless me, O bless me! Give me land, large tracts of land. And provide your personal protection—don't let evil hurt me." God gave him what he asked." (1 Chronicles 4:10, MSG)

Jabez entered the world under painful circumstances, bringing great sorrow to his mother, who gave him a name that reflected her suffering—"sorrow, pain, suffering." Imagine the weight Jabez must have felt each time his name was spoken, a constant reminder of hardship that wasn't his fault. His name carried a heavy connotation, symbolizing failure and defeat. But Jabez refused to let his name dictate his destiny. He knew that God's blessings could rewrite his story.

With a heart full of faith, Jabez turned to the God of Israel, praying earnestly for a transformation. He boldly asked for blessings, for an increase in land, and for divine protection from harm and evil. In His limitless grace, God heard Jabez's prayer and answered it, blessing him abundantly and safeguarding his future.

Jabez's story is a reminder that God's power to bless and transform is not limited to a select few. The same God who worked in Jabez's life is present and willing to work in yours. No matter the weight of labels, circumstances, or challenges, God has the power to change your story.

Take inspiration from Jabez's bold faith. Seek the Lord's blessings with confidence, trusting in His love and provision. Aim high in your prayers, knowing that God's plans for you are greater than you can imagine. Just as He did for Jabez, God can do the extraordinary in your life. Let your prayers reflect your trust in His limitless power.

Week 12 Wednesday

He Can Do The Impossible!

"Jesus looked at them intently and said, "Humanly speaking, it is impossible. But with God everything is possible." (Matthew 19:26, NLT)

While we often navigate life balancing both our emotional and logical sides, many of us lean toward logic, especially when faced with challenges that seem impossible. Logic helps us rely on facts, tangible resources, and what feels within reach. Yet, it's vital to pause and reflect on a higher power—what God can do. Have His abilities ever known limits?

Throughout history, God has revealed His boundless power in awe-inspiring ways: parting the Red Sea, sending fire from the heavens, healing the sick, and even raising the dead. These acts serve as reminders that His capabilities far surpass our natural understanding.

When we limit ourselves to reasoning alone, we miss out on the extraordinary. Stepping into faith means acknowledging the supernatural and trusting that God can work in ways we could never foresee. It's in these moments of trust, especially when life's challenges feel overwhelming, that we allow space for faith to transform our reality.

By leaning on God and letting go of doubt, we open our hearts to witness miracles—where the impossible becomes possible. So today, let's choose to trust Him wholeheartedly. Let's invite His power to work in our lives and rest in the assurance that with God, nothing is beyond reach. Trust Him, and watch how faith changes everything.

Week 12 Thursday

Chose Joy!

"You have put more joy in my heart than they have when their grain and wine abound." (Psalm 4:7, ESV)

Too often, our minds are consumed by what lies ahead—achieving goals, reaching milestones, or preparing for the next chapter of life. While looking toward the future can drive us, it can also steal the simple joys that exist right now. The beauty of life often rests in the present, but we miss it when we're too focused on what's next.

Life's challenges and obstacles may try to pull us into worry and fear, but even in the hardest moments, joy can be found. It begins with grounding ourselves in the here and now, letting go of what we can't control, and choosing gratitude for the little things that make each day special. A gentle breeze, a kind word, or even a moment of stillness can remind us of life's blessings.

By anchoring ourselves in today, we allow our minds to work with us rather than against us. Joy isn't something we need to search for—it already resides within us, waiting to be embraced. All it takes is a shift in focus and the willingness to celebrate life's small victories.

So, let's choose joy. Let's breathe deeply, savor the moment, and embrace each day as a precious gift. The present is where life truly happens, and it's far too valuable to overlook. Trust in its beauty, and you'll find happiness waiting for you right where you are.

Week 12 Friday

Appreciate Others!

"Let nothing be done through selfish ambition or conceit, but in lowliness of mind let each esteem others better than himself." (Philippians 2:3, NKJV)

In a world that often glorifies self-centeredness, we're reminded of a higher calling—to set aside selfish ambition and conceit and instead embrace humility by placing others above ourselves. It's not always easy, but it's a reflection of the heart of God. To esteem others means to hold them in high regard, honoring their value by putting their needs before our own.

Jesus lived this out beautifully during His time on Earth, consistently showing us what it means to value others as God's masterpieces. Each person, no matter their flaws, carries an inherent worth that God Himself recognizes. Though they may not always express it, every individual is deserving of love, respect, and honor.

We all long to feel valued and acknowledged. But this starts with us—by sowing seeds of kindness and appreciation, we create a ripple effect of love and honor that touches lives and often comes back to us. A simple word of encouragement or a heartfelt gesture can profoundly impact someone's day.

Today, take a moment to reach out to someone. Send a text, make a call, or share a word of gratitude that lets them know how much they mean to you. By lifting others up, we reflect God's love and embody the humility He calls us to. Let's make space in our hearts for kindness, knowing that small acts of love can spark lasting joy in the lives of those around us.

Week 13 Monday

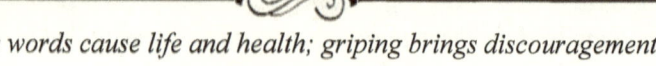
Life and Health

"Gentle words cause life and health; griping brings discouragement."
(Proverbs 15:4, TLB)

Did you know that God has given each of us a beautiful gift—the ability to bring joy and encouragement to those around us, especially our loved ones? It's not tied to hard work, education, wealth, fame, or worldly achievements. Instead, it's found in something far more powerful: the words we choose to speak.

Scripture tells us, "Gentle words cause life and health." These words are more than just kind gestures—they carry the power to breathe life into someone's heart, restoring their spirit and well-being. Those closest to you need to feel your care, but even more than that, they need to *hear* it. They need to hear that they are loved, that their efforts matter, and that their abilities inspire pride and belief in them.

Too often, we wait until it's too late—expressing love only in moments of loss. But what if we made it a daily practice to pour life into our relationships through gentle, loving words? Our encouragement can build others up and bring vitality to their lives in ways we may never fully realize.

Why not take the opportunity today to reach out to someone you care about? A simple text, a kind word, or a heartfelt call can mean the world to them. Let them know how much you love and value them. With God's gift of words, you have the power to bring joy and strength to those you hold dear—today and every day.

Week 13 Tuesday

A Planned Destiny!

"Be alert and of sober mind. Your enemy the devil prowls around like a roaring lion looking for someone to devour." (1 Peter 5:8, NIV)

Easter beautifully reminds us of the incredible sacrifice Jesus made for humanity through His crucifixion and resurrection. The enemy once believed that killing Jesus would erase God's presence on earth. Yet, unbeknownst to him, it was all part of God's divine plan—an act of love and redemption that would change everything. Jesus willingly bore the weight of our sins, paid the ultimate price for our salvation, and triumphed over death, rising victoriously.

Although the devil still prowls, seeking to deceive and intimidate, he has been stripped of his true power by Jesus' sacrifice. The devil is not the roaring lion he pretends to be; he cannot compel, defeat, control, or determine the destiny God has lovingly prepared for us. Our future rests safely in God's hands, and as we trust Him and align our lives with His purpose, we discover a path filled with hope, peace, and meaning.

The enemy may try to distract or derail us, whispering doubt and fear into our hearts. Yet, Easter reminds us of an unshakable truth: God's plan is always greater. With faith in Him, we can stand firm, knowing that no obstacle is too great for His love to overcome. Let this season inspire us to trust in His perfect will, celebrate His victorious sacrifice, and embrace the abundant life He has gifted us. May we walk confidently in the destiny shaped by His loving hands.

Week 13 Wednesday

Thoughts and Feelings

"You keep him in perfect peace whose mind is stayed on you, because he trusts in you." (Isaiah 26:3, ESV)

Each day, our minds create memories, thoughts, and feelings—some of which can uplift us, while others weigh us down. At times, our thoughts and emotions become limiting, bringing fears, worries, anxieties, and doubts into our hearts. Yet, scripture offers us a powerful reminder: when we fix our minds on God, He promises us perfect peace.

This peace comes when we place our trust fully in Him. When our thoughts are centered on God, negativity begins to fade, replaced by hope, purpose, and a renewed sense of self-worth. We become open to His favor and blessings, paving the way for breakthroughs that only He can provide.

Too often, we allow our circumstances to consume us, pulling us away from the present joys and the community of faith. Fixating on our struggles can drain the vibrancy from our lives and leave us feeling isolated. But when we lift our gaze to God, we remember a vital truth: our thoughts and emotions do not define or change who God is.

Let's choose to let go of the distractions that hold us back. Instead, let's keep our hearts focused on Him. By turning to God with trust and gratitude, we can embrace His peace and walk confidently in His promises. Today, let's fix our minds on His goodness and rejoice in the strength and blessings He provides. God is unchanging, and His love will always guide us forward.

Week 13 Thursday

The Need For Self-Care!

"Then Jesus said, "Let's go off by ourselves to a quiet place and rest awhile." He said this because there were so many people coming and going that Jesus and his apostles didn't even have time to eat." (Mark 6:31, NLT)

Jesus was a perfect example of living a life dedicated to doing good. He healed the sick, performed miracles, shared teachings, traveled tirelessly, and invested deeply in His disciples. Wherever He went, crowds followed Him, seeking His time, energy, and presence. Yet amidst His busy and demanding schedule, Jesus recognized the importance of self-care. He understood the need to pause, step away, and renew Himself, setting a powerful example for His disciples and all of us.

Even as the Son of God, filled with boundless power, wisdom, blessings, and anointing, Jesus knew the significance of resting and avoiding burnout—both spiritual and physical. This shows us that no matter how spiritually strong, mentally equipped, or physically capable we may be, taking intentional time for ourselves is essential.

In our own lives, self-care allows us to refresh and realign, enabling us to be more effective and present in everything we do. It's not selfish; it's an act of wisdom and love—for ourselves and those we care for. Let's follow Jesus' example by stepping away from the demands of life, even briefly, to recuperate and rejuvenate.

Today, make it a priority to take some "me" time. Whether through quiet reflection, prayer, or simply resting, allow yourself the space to renew your strength and embrace peace. Just as Jesus cared for Himself, let's honor this practice and be reminded that self-care is a vital part of a purposeful and fulfilling life.

Week 13 Friday

Do Not Resist!

"But Jesus said, "Don't resist anymore." (Luke 22:51, TLB)

As Jesus prepared to be arrested and crucified, He made a profound statement that continues to inspire us today. When the soldiers came for Him, Peter, in an attempt to defend both Jesus and himself, struck one of them, cutting off his ear. Yet in an act of incredible mercy, Jesus healed the man's ear, leaving no evidence for Peter to be accused. Though the betrayal, false accusations, trial, and crucifixion were undeniably wrong, Jesus embraced them, knowing they were essential to fulfilling His divine purpose.

The soldiers, religious leaders, disciples—no one could see that these wrongs were all part of God's plan, necessary to lead Jesus to the cross. It was not the enemy guiding these events, but God Himself directing them toward redemption. While human behavior played a role, it was ultimately God's hand ensuring His plan unfolded perfectly.

This teaches us a vital lesson: when faced with difficult situations, we must resist the urge to fight back, worry, or become distracted. Instead, we are called to trust God and stay focused on what is right. Even when life feels chaotic, God holds our destiny firmly in His hands.

Take heart and believe that His plans for you are greater than any challenge or obstacle. Keep your focus on Him, and you will see His faithfulness as He leads you through every trial and into the victory He has prepared. With God, a way forward is always waiting.

Week 14 Monday

Focus On The 99!

"...whatever is pure and wholesome, whatever is lovely and brings peace, whatever is admirable and of good repute; if there is any excellence, if there is anything worthy of praise, think continually on these things."
(Philippians 4:8, AMP)

It's fascinating that the apostle Paul, in Philippians 4:8, AMP, uses the word "if"—a word that implies possibility and hope. He writes, *"If there is any excellence, if there is anything worthy of praise, think continually on these things."* This reminds us of the importance of shifting our focus toward the good in others, especially those closest to us—our children, spouses, friends, or anyone God has placed in our lives.

Instead of fixating on the one flaw, mistake, or wrong choice someone may have made, we're called to notice and celebrate the 99 good qualities they possess. Far too often, our minds naturally gravitate toward criticism or judgment, overlooking the beauty and excellence that reside within each person. By focusing on their goodness and giving praise where it's due, we reflect God's heart.

None of us are perfect, and it's easy to get discouraged when loved ones fall short or make choices we may not agree with. However, we're reminded to see others through God's eyes—acknowledging their worth, potential, and the goodness they bring into our lives. This mindset not only honors them but also brings peace and joy to our own hearts.

Let's make it a daily practice to intentionally dwell on what is excellent and praiseworthy in those around us.

Week 14 Tuesday

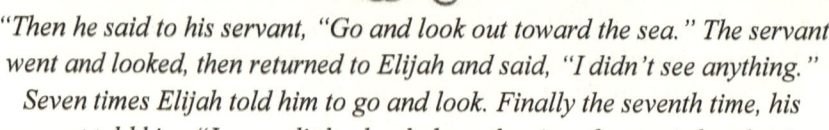
Facts, Realities & God

"Then he said to his servant, "Go and look out toward the sea." The servant went and looked, then returned to Elijah and said, "I didn't see anything." Seven times Elijah told him to go and look. Finally the seventh time, his servant told him, "I saw a little cloud about the size of a man's hand rising from the sea." (1 Kings 18:43–44, NLT)

Elijah, the prophet, boldly told King Ahab that rain was on its way to end the three-year drought. While Elijah prayed, he sent his assistant to look for signs of rain, relying on him to report back. Time after time—six times, in fact—the assistant returned with disappointing news: "I didn't see anything." While his words were truthful and reflected the current reality, they could have easily discouraged Elijah.

This story reminds us that even those closest to us, with the best of intentions, may sometimes speak from a place of facts that seem to oppose the blessings we're believing for. But when God has spoken to your heart, hold on to His promises with unwavering faith. Elijah could have given up after hearing "nothing" so many times, but he remained steadfast, praying and trusting in what God had revealed. Finally, on the seventh attempt, there was a small yet unmistakable sign of rain.

Don't let others' doubts, even when grounded in facts, shake your belief in what God has promised you. His word always prevails over natural circumstances. Keep trusting, keep praying, and keep believing—your breakthrough is closer than you think!

Week 14 Wednesday

A Lifetime Commitment!

"I will be your God throughout your lifetime—until your hair is white with age. I made you, and I will care for you. I will carry you along and save you."
(Isaiah 46:4, NLT)

God's promise to us is unwavering: He will walk beside us through every moment of our lives, encompassing every season—whether joyful, challenging, or uncertain. In the moments of triumph, He celebrates with us. In the times of hardship, when we feel the weight of the world pressing down, He carries us, offering His grace, strength, wisdom, and peace to see us through.

This promise is not temporary but eternal. It is His covenant to remain by our side until the end of our earthly journey. Along the way, God gently guides us, ordering our steps and pouring His favor into our lives. Like the light of a North Star, His blessings illuminate the path ahead, enabling us to thrive even amid trials.

Wherever you find yourself today—whether in a place of hope or struggle—take comfort in the unchanging truth that you are never alone. God's loving presence surrounds you, and His plan for you is filled with hope and goodness. Trust that He holds your life in His capable hands, working all things for your ultimate good.

Let His promise fill your heart with courage and peace as you move forward, knowing He is your steadfast guide, your source of strength, and your refuge. God is with you, through it all, always.

Week 14 Thursday

Jesus Reacted To A Touch.

"She had heard the reports concerning Jesus, and she came up behind Him in the throng and touched His garment, for she kept saying, If I only touch His garments, I shall be restored to health." (Mark 5:27–28, AMPC)

This is the story of a woman who suffered from a bleeding disorder for twelve long years. She had heard about Jesus and, with unwavering determination in her heart, believed that if she could just touch the hem of His garment, she would be healed. Scripture tells us that the moment she reached out and touched Him, she was instantly healed, and Jesus felt power flow from Him.

Many of us carry unseen wounds, emotionally bleeding from challenges that have drained us for years. It might be struggles with work, finances, relationships, health, mental well-being, or feelings of insecurity, doubt, and low self-esteem. These issues disrupt our lives and weigh heavily on our hearts. Yet, like the woman in this story, we are reminded to approach Jesus with determination and faith.

Even small steps toward Him can lead to life-changing breakthroughs. Push through whatever is holding you back—fear, doubt, or hardship—just as the woman pushed through the crowd, refusing to let anything stop her. The moment she touched Jesus, she received her miracle.

Your miracle is waiting for you too. Take that step of faith, draw closer to Him, and trust in His power to heal, restore, and bring new life to your circumstances. He is ready to meet you right where you are.

Week 14 Friday

Only For A While!

"God is our refuge and strength, a very present help in trouble."
(Psalm 46:1, NKJV)

Reading this verse has stirred deep emotions, reminding me of the darkest seasons I've endured. There were times when life's relentless storms weighed heavily on me, leaving me feeling trapped with no escape in sight. The challenges were overwhelming, and there were moments I teetered on the edge of despair. Though I knew God was with me, the pain often felt endless, draining me of hope and strength.

Yet, as the storm clouds eventually cleared, I began to see the breakthrough—a glimpse of God's divine purpose behind it all. Each trial was not without meaning; God had orchestrated every step to refine and grow me. He tailored the challenges to my strength, standing by me as a faithful ally in my weakest moments. What the enemy intended for harm, God transformed into blessings beyond anything I could have imagined. He became my refuge and my strength, turning my mourning into dancing and rewarding my perseverance with His abundant grace and favor.

Let this serve as a gentle reminder: even in moments when we feel utterly alone, God's presence surrounds us. He is guiding us through every hardship, working all things for our good. Trust in Him, and you will witness how He brings light to even the darkest of times. His faithfulness never fails.

Week 15 Monday

Jesus Took The Evidence

"But Jesus said, "No more of this." And he touched the man's ear and healed him." (Luke 22:51, NLT)

This story takes place as Jesus prepared to be arrested. In an attempt to defend Him, Simon Peter drew his sword and struck Malchus, the high priest's servant, cutting off his ear. Yet, in an extraordinary act of mercy, Jesus healed Malchus's ear. Have you ever wondered why Jesus performed this healing?

Striking Malchus's ear wasn't just a physical act—it symbolized punishment and humiliation, effectively ostracizing him from temple service and society. By restoring his ear, Jesus ensured there would be no evidence against Peter. This act protected Peter, shielding him from accusation and harm.

This moment mirrors what Jesus accomplished for us on the cross. He didn't just heal physical wounds; He removed every piece of evidence the enemy could hold against us. By His sacrifice, He washed away our sins, casting them as far as the East is from the West and into the sea of forgetfulness. His boundless mercy shows us why serving the Lord is a calling worth embracing.

Even Peter, who denied Jesus three times, grew in faith and went on to change the world. His story is a reminder that failure doesn't define us. Like Peter, we can move forward with courage and determination, trusting God's transformative power. Let's adopt Peter's bold attitude, embrace God's grace, and live lives of purpose and faith!

Week 15 Tuesday

Self-Value and Self-Worth

"I praise you because I am fearfully and wonderfully made." (Psalm 139:14, NIV)

One of life's most significant challenges is overcoming fear. Many of us struggle to see our true self-value and self-worth, failing to recognize ourselves through the lens of God's boundless love. Yet, it is vital to acknowledge the inherent strengths, spiritual resilience, and unlimited potential that He has placed within each of us.

The enemy often seeks to distort our self-perception, planting seeds of doubt and insecurity. But we must hold fast to the truth that we are fearfully and wonderfully made—each one of us a masterpiece, lovingly crafted by God. Instead of allowing negative thoughts to take root, let's align our minds with His truth, affirming His purpose for our lives.

Just as we joyfully celebrate our children, God takes immense delight in us. He sees our worth, even when we struggle to see it ourselves. The doubts that invade our minds are simply distractions designed to steer us away from embracing the immeasurable value given to us by our Creator.

Today, let's reject fear and negativity and speak life into our hearts. Use positive affirmations grounded in God's truth, reminding yourself of the unique and cherished being He has shaped you to be. Rest in the knowledge that you are deeply loved, celebrated, and called to live a life of purpose and confidence through His grace.

Week 15 Wednesday

Royalty Blood

"Mephibosheth bowed to David again and said, "You are being very kind to me, your servant! And I am no better than a dead dog!" (2 Samuel 9:8, NCV)

Mephibosheth, the grandson of King Saul, endured a difficult life after Saul, Jonathan, and his father were killed in battle. Left alone and crippled from an accident, he spent many years in the slums of Lo-Debar, with nothing to his name. His hardships led him to compare himself to a dog, allowing his circumstances to define his identity and forgetting his noble lineage.

However, King David saw beyond Mephibosheth's struggles and remembered who he truly was. With compassion and grace, David brought Mephibosheth to the palace, restoring all that had belonged to his grandfather. This act reminds us that no matter how lost or broken we may feel, our identity is anchored in something greater.

Like Mephibosheth, many of us forget that we carry royal blood within us. Through adoption into the Kingdom of Heaven, we are sons and daughters of God. Yet, life's challenges and circumstances often cloud this truth, leading us to see ourselves through the lens of our struggles instead of God's love.

It's time to reclaim our identity in Christ. Let's rise above our circumstances and remember who we are—fearfully and wonderfully made, cherished, and empowered by God. We are heirs of His Kingdom, called to live in the fullness of His promises. Hold tightly to this truth, for your value and worth are found in Him. Let His love define you, not your challenges.

Week 15 Thursday

The Right Timing

"So let's not get tired of doing what is good. At just the right time we will reap a harvest of blessing if we don't give up." (Galatians 6:9, NLT)

What a beautiful and timely reminder. Many of us devote ourselves to doing good, only to feel disheartened when the changes we long for seem slow to come. Progress may feel invisible, and the temptation to give up or shift focus can be strong. Yet, it's essential to remember this profound truth: God's timing is perfect. He is never late, and His plans for us far surpass what we could imagine.

Even when we can't see it, God is working behind the scenes, preparing something extraordinary. He's aligning situations, refining our paths, and connecting us with the right people so that His blessings and favor can unfold in their fullness. The delays we experience aren't denials; they're part of His divine process.

Scripture encourages us not to grow weary in doing good, reminding us that perseverance is the key. When we stay focused and stable in our faith, we position ourselves to reap a beautiful harvest of blessings—if we refuse to give up. Waiting is often the hardest part, but it's also where God's grace grows us the most.

Today, take heart and trust in His perfect timing. The season of harvest is coming, and when it does, the blessings will far outweigh the waiting. God holds every moment in His hands, and He will bring forth His best for you in due time. Keep pressing on, knowing that His plan is always worth the wait.

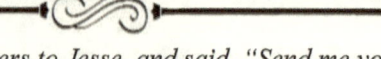

Something Valuable

"Therefore Saul sent messengers to Jesse, and said, "Send me your son David, who is with the sheep." (1 Samuel 16:19, NKJV)

King Saul was tormented by depression and spiritual attacks. Despite being a king with access to anything he could ever need—doctors, therapists, and the finest musicians—none could bring him relief. What Saul truly needed was the presence of God, carried by none other than David, a humble shepherd boy.

Even Saul's staff recognized David's gift and suggested he come to play for the king. Yet when the message was sent, it wasn't addressed to David—it was sent to Jesse, his father. Jesse, who had previously failed to see David's value, overlooked him when the prophet Samuel came to anoint one of his sons as king. Left out in the fields to tend sheep, David was dismissed as unworthy.

But now, with the king's officials standing at his door requesting David, Jesse could no longer deny his son's worth. This moment was a powerful reminder of David's significance—not just in the eyes of men, but in the eyes of God. David's value wasn't determined by his position or others' opinions; it was rooted in his connection with God.

This story challenges us to appreciate those who carry the presence of God, especially those closest to us. Sometimes, like Jesse, we may fail to recognize their worth. But let's not miss the opportunity to honor and cherish them for the blessings they bring. Value the Davids in your life—they may be the ones through whom God's presence flows most profoundly.

Week 16 Monday

Planning Something!

"Be glad for all God is planning for you. Be patient in trouble, and prayerful always." (Romans 12:12, TLB)

Life's journey can often feel frustrating, especially when we're striving to grow and improve, only to feel like progress is slow or nonexistent. Some days, we may feel stuck, like we're treading water. Other times, it might seem as though each step forward is followed by two steps back. And for some, the spark to even try may feel dim or completely out of reach. These moments can leave us feeling discouraged and weary.

Yet, Romans 12:12 (TLB) reminds us to remain joyful in the plans God has for us, patient through life's trials, and steadfast in prayer. God's plans are not just good—they are perfect, and they are designed to lead us into a brighter future. Even the challenges we face, though difficult, serve as stepping stones to shape and prepare us for His purpose. Where the enemy intends harm, God transforms it for our good, using every hardship to bless us in ways we cannot yet see.

In those moments when progress feels slow, we are called to trust in His perfect timing. His plans are never delayed, and nothing happens by chance. When we lean into patience and stay connected to Him through prayer, we open our hearts to peace and His unfailing guidance.

Wherever you are on your journey, take heart—God is faithfully working in your life, paving the way for blessings yet to come. Hold on, stay prayerful, and trust in His perfect purpose. Your breakthrough is on its way.

Week 16 Tuesday

Be An Overcomer!

"Who is it that overcomes the world? Only the one who believes that Jesus is the Son of God." (1 John 5:5, NIV)

We are reminded that our ability to accomplish is directly tied to how much we're willing to push ourselves forward. Achieving greatness in any area of life is like learning a new language—the more we invest our hearts and souls into it, the more fluent and confident we become.

We are called "overcomers" when we believe Jesus is the Son of God and embrace the confidence to pursue our fullest potential. Yet, many of us, though blessed with incredible talents, gifts, favor, and good positions in life, often feel stuck. We lose sight of visions and dreams, trapped in ruts of behaviors, addictions, or bad habits that hold us back.

God desires for us to rise above these barriers. He calls us to overcome the limitations of the "world"—anything that restricts or slows our progress. We are encouraged to love others with extraordinary passion, to work harder than ever before, and to show kindness in ways that leave a lasting impact. Take time to connect deeply with those you cherish, and refuse to let any obstacle stand between you and the purpose God has placed on your life.

You are an overcomer! Push past what holds you back, trusting in the strength God provides, and step boldly into the abundant life He has called you to live. Let His truth guide you, and victory will be yours.

Week 16 Wednesday

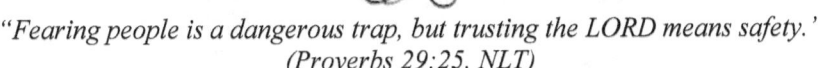
A God Pleaser!

"Fearing people is a dangerous trap, but trusting the LORD means safety."
(Proverbs 29:25, NLT)

For many of us, fear becomes a constant companion throughout life. We battle social anxiety, worrying about others' opinions, and, in our effort to avoid conflict, we may find ourselves becoming doormats, sacrificing our own peace to please others. Seeking validation from people can feel like a heavy burden, and yet, it's not the approval of others that defines us. God calls us to be "God pleasers," not "people pleasers."

Scripture reminds us, *"Fearing people is a dangerous trap, but trusting the LORD means safety."* When we place our trust in God, we discover a true sense of safety and purpose that people's opinions can never provide. Trusting in Him frees us from distractions and sets our hearts firmly on His plans for our lives.

It's easy to let fear and doubt derail us from our destiny. Yet, those who trust in the Lord are marked by His love and favor. Though the path may feel lonely at times, the rewards of trusting Him are immeasurable. His guidance brings clarity, and His promises anchor us in hope.

Today, let go of the need for others' approval and rest in God's love. Trust Him wholeheartedly, and you'll uncover the meaningful, secure life He's designed for you. Your destiny is waiting—step forward in faith, knowing He is with you every step of the way.

Week 16 Thursday

Jesus Healed Them

"Great crowds came to Jesus, bringing with them the lame, the blind, the crippled, those who could not speak, and many others. They put them at Jesus' feet, and he healed them." (Matthew 15:30, NCV)

People often turn to doctors seeking solutions to the physical, mental, or emotional struggles they face. These challenges—whether stress, anxiety, or deeper psychological issues—can feel overwhelming. Yet, scripture tells us that great crowds flocked to Jesus, drawn by His extraordinary power. They witnessed Him perform miracles that even the most skilled doctors of the time couldn't fathom: healing the lame, the blind, the crippled, the mute, and countless others.

But who were these "many others"? Could they have been individuals wrestling with depression, anxiety, or other mental afflictions? Could they have included those facing broken marriages, financial hardships, or feeling trapped in darkness and despair? Perhaps they were people who felt as if they'd reached the end of their rope, desperate for hope and healing.

The remarkable truth is that everyone who came to Jesus was healed. He extended His touch to each one, offering them new life and restoration. He is the same compassionate Savior today as He was then. No matter what challenges or struggles you are facing—physical, emotional, or spiritual—Jesus is ready to heal and make a way. His love knows no limits, and His power brings hope where none seems possible.

Take heart and trust in Him. Just as He healed the crowds then, He can bring healing and peace to your life today. His arms are open, waiting to restore and guide you forward.

Week 16 Friday

See The Goodness of God

"I recall the many miracles he did for me so long ago. Those wonderful deeds are constantly in my thoughts. I cannot stop thinking about them."
(Psalm 77:11–12, TLB)

We have a beautiful responsibility to renew our minds and reshape our thinking to cultivate gratitude for the goodness of God. It's far too easy to fixate on the one wrong thing rather than the countless blessings in our lives and the lives of those around us. Negative thoughts often carry more weight than positive ones, which is why we need daily reminders—positive affirmations—to lift our spirits and keep us smiling.

The Psalmist's secret to resilience was focusing on the goodness of God. This gave him strength to face battles and overcome life's challenges. We are called to do the same. Let's reflect on His blessings and favor in our lives, the ways He has protected us and our loved ones from dangers both seen and unseen, and the provision He has poured out—through finances, jobs, education, or even the simplest moments like shopping. Think of how God has surrounded you with the right people at just the right time and how, no matter the hardship, things could have been far worse without His hand upon your life.

Today, pause and intentionally dwell on God's goodness. Let His faithfulness fill your heart with gratitude and joy. The more we focus on His blessings, the more we'll see how His love and favor transform our lives in ways beyond measure. Take a moment to celebrate His goodness and let it strengthen your spirit for the journey ahead.

Week 17 Monday

Never Stop Believing!

"It had been revealed to him by the Holy Spirit that he would not die before he had seen the Lord's Messiah." (Luke 2:26, NIV)

This scripture reminds us beautifully that God prepares us for things that have yet to unfold. Though we don't know how long Simeon had held onto the revelation given to him by the Holy Spirit, we do know that he waited faithfully, trusting in God's promise—even when no sign of the Messiah appeared. Like anyone, Simeon likely faced moments of doubt, with the enemy planting negative thoughts to challenge what he believed. But Simeon remained steadfast, anticipating each day with hope, expecting to see the fulfillment of God's word.

When the moment finally came, and Simeon met Jesus as a newborn in the temple, he *knew*. The promise became reality, igniting his faith. That encounter didn't just strengthen Simeon—it became a testimony that built the faith of those around him. His unwavering trust in God's promise became a source of encouragement for many.

We too are called to hold tightly to what God has spoken over our lives. His word is filled with promises like "I can do all things through Christ," "lay hands on the sick and they shall recover," "ask anything," and "signs and wonders shall follow those who believe." These truths remind us that God's promises are unchanging and His plans are perfect.

No matter what doubts or delays we face, let us never stop believing. Trust in His timing, hold fast to His word, and know that what He has promised will come to pass. Stay encouraged, and let your faith shine.

Week 17 Tuesday

Always With Us!

"Therefore put on the full armor of God, so that when the day of evil comes, you may be able to stand your ground, and after you have done everything, to stand." (Ephesians 6:13, NIV)

The Bible's call to put on the whole armor of God is a powerful reminder that we will face battles in life. These challenges may come as attacks meant to slow us down, distract us, or weaken our faith. God never promised a life free of problems, trials, or attacks from the enemy. However, He did promise that He would never allow us to bear more than we can handle. He is faithful to walk with us through every trial, shielding us as we face the enemy's fiery darts.

God's promises are unwavering. He assures us of His protection, preparing a table for us even in the presence of our enemies. He becomes our shelter and stronghold, guiding us through every difficulty. What the enemy intends for harm, God transforms into opportunities to strengthen our faith, build character, and cultivate maturity. Every trial becomes part of His greater plan to shape us into the image of Jesus.

When challenges arise, remember that God's hand is on your life. Stay steadfast in your faith, trusting in His promises. He is working behind the scenes, aligning everything for your breakthrough.

No matter how hard the battle feels, know that God is with you. He is your refuge, your strength, and your source of hope. Keep your faith strong and your eyes fixed on Him. Your victory is on the horizon, and His love will carry you through. Trust in His timing and take heart—your breakthrough is coming!

Week 17 Wednesday

The Doorway To Healing!

"He has sent me to bind up the brokenhearted... to bestow on them a crown of beauty instead of ashes... " (Isaiah 61:1,3, NIV)

The Bible's clear mention that Jesus came to heal the broken-hearted reveals God's deep awareness of the pain many of us carry. While some may openly express their hurt, others mask their struggles behind a facade of smiles, quietly battling negative thoughts and inner turmoil. No matter how pain manifests, God's love is unchanging, and His desire to bring healing is unwavering.

We need to remember that God's love runs deeper than we can fathom. He sees our worth and significance, even when we struggle to see it ourselves. His compassionate heart longs to replace our sorrows with a crown of beauty, showing just how deeply He cares for each of us. This promise is a powerful reminder of the transformation that comes when we lean into His love.

Healing begins with transparency. When we are vulnerable and honest before the Lord, we open the doorway to restoration. God is ready to mend the brokenness of our past, but He waits for us to take that first step—to desire healing and choose to move forward. This choice is an act of faith, trusting Him to lead us out of pain and into the fullness of life.

Today, let go of the weight of sorrow and embrace the healing Jesus offers. His love holds the power to restore what has been lost, to bring peace to our hearts, and to renew our spirits. God's arms are open, inviting us to trust Him, surrender our pain, and find lasting hope in His promises. Your healing is waiting—take the step toward Him.

Week 17 Thursday

Victory Through Christ!

"No, despite all these things, overwhelming victory is ours through Christ, who loved us." (Romans 8:37, NLT)

We find immense comfort in this scripture, knowing that God desires for us to develop spiritual resilience that brings stability and joy even in the midst of life's challenges. His promises remind us that our victories are not distant dreams, but tangible realities for all who believe and place their trust in Him.

No matter how overwhelming the obstacles may seem, we can stand firm in the assurance of victory through our faith in Christ. His unwavering love surrounds us, empowering us to overcome adversity and walk boldly through life's struggles. With Christ, we are far more than survivors—we are conquerors, triumphing over trials and tribulations with the strength He provides.

Through Him, we find an unshakable source of courage and perseverance. He equips us to face life's challenges with grace, transforming what feels impossible into opportunities for growth and deeper trust in Him. By His power, we can navigate each hardship with renewed hope, knowing He is our steadfast guide.

Let this truth encourage your heart today: Christ's love never fails, and His victory is your victory. Lean into His presence, embrace His promises, and trust that even in the hardest moments, He is working for your good. With Him by your side, you can find the strength to overcome and the peace to move forward with confidence. Your triumph in Him is already assured!

Week 17 Friday

Lavish Attention

"He found him out in the wilderness, in an empty, windswept wasteland. He threw his arms around him, lavished attention on him, guarding him as the apple of his eye." (Deuteronomy 32:10, MSG)

The "wilderness" symbolizes a dry, barren place where nothing seems to thrive—a space many of us may find ourselves in during certain seasons of life. It's where, despite all our efforts and doing the right things, progress feels out of reach. Finances may remain tight, health struggles may linger without improvement, and relationships may feel stagnant or unfulfilled. Some of us face challenges with our children, who seem to disregard their path and make poor choices, leaving us feeling helpless and burdened. These "wilderness" experiences can feel confining, as though life's circumstances have us stuck.

Yet, it is in these very moments of struggle that God's presence is most profound. Scripture reminds us that God meets us right where we are—even in the barren wilderness. He sees us in the empty, windswept wasteland, and He does not turn away. Instead, He draws close, embracing us with His love, lavishing us with His attention, and protecting us as the apple of His eye.

No matter how desolate or challenging your wilderness feels, take heart. You are not forgotten, and you are not alone. God is on your side, working in ways you may not yet see. Trust that He is walking alongside you, guiding you through, and preparing you for what lies ahead. His promises remain steadfast, and His love will carry you through every dry season. Stay encouraged—your breakthrough is coming.

Week 18 Monday

Don't Be Intimidated

"O Lord, please hear my prayer! Listen to the prayers of those of us who delight in honoring you. Please grant me success today by making the king favorable to me. Put it into his heart to be kind to me." (Nehemiah 1:11, NLT)

Nehemiah had a heartfelt desire to see the walls and gates of Jerusalem restored, a vision born out of his love for his city and its people. As the king's cupbearer, he held a trusted but humble position—far from one of prominence or influence. He lacked experience in building, the manpower to execute such a monumental task, and the resources to make it happen. But Nehemiah had something even greater: faith in the power of prayer.

He prayed boldly, asking God to grant him favor in approaching the king and to stir the king's heart to support him. Nehemiah didn't let fear or doubt cloud his faith. The king responded favorably, granting Nehemiah everything he needed—resources, permission, and even manpower to accomplish the task.

Nehemiah's story teaches us a powerful lesson: we should never be intimidated by the enormity of our dreams. God doesn't plant big dreams in the hearts of those who think small. Instead, He calls us to trust Him and step out in faith. The dreams in your heart are there for a reason—because you are created for greatness. You are a world-changer, a history-maker, and a successor to God's promises.

So, pray boldly. Believe that God will open doors, provide resources, and guide your steps. Dream big and trust that with God, nothing is impossible. He will equip you for the vision He has placed within you and bring it to fruition in His perfect timing. Step into your calling with courage—greatness awaits!

Week 18 Tuesday

Doubts Can Cheat

"Elijah went before the people and said, "How long will you waver between two opinions?" (1 Kings 18:21, NIV)

We often find ourselves caught between two worlds, wrestling with doubts and fears as we face decisions. Some of us may lean on the phrase, "I'm waiting to hear from the Lord," as we hesitate to act. But God's word is a guiding light, encouraging us to trust Him and move forward with the desires He has placed on our hearts. It is in those moments when His call diverges from societal norms that we encounter some of the greatest challenges—whether it's stepping out in generosity, engaging with someone who makes us uncomfortable, humbling ourselves to apologize, offering forgiveness, letting go of the past, or making bold, faith-driven choices.

The key is to safeguard our minds. Negative thoughts and doubts can hinder us from embracing opportunities meant to bless us and bring us closer to God's purpose for our lives. This is why believing in God's word is absolutely essential. He calls us to trust Him wholeheartedly, knowing that His promises are true and His plans are always for our good.

Whatever challenges you're facing today, let this be the moment you step out in faith. Release your doubts, silence negative thoughts, and embrace the opportunities God has set before you.

Believing in His word and taking action allows His power to work through you, transforming hesitation into progress and fear into faith. Today, trust in His voice, follow His lead, and take that bold step forward—you are never alone, and His plans for you are full of hope and promise!

Week 18 Wednesday

Celebrate Your Challenges!

"By this I know that You are well pleased with me, because my enemy does not triumph over me." (Psalm 41:11, NKJV)

Scripture reminds us that God's favor is not defined by the battles He shields us from, but by His steadfast presence and guidance as we walk through them. David understood this deeply, having experienced God's triumph over his enemies during some of the darkest and most challenging times in his life. Instead of dwelling on his defeats, David chose to focus on the victories God had secured for him, finding strength and hope in God's faithfulness.

This truth encourages us to persevere in our own moments of adversity. No matter how difficult the circumstances, we can take heart in knowing that God will not abandon us. He is with us in every storm, working to bring joy and purpose even in the midst of trials. Like David, we can push forward, trusting that God will see us through.

When we feel attacked or overwhelmed, we can rely on His presence to carry us. God's promise is sure—He will never leave us to face our challenges alone. His strength is our refuge, and His love is unshakable.

David's words inspire us to declare the same: *"By this I know that You are well pleased with me, because my enemy does not triumph over me."* Let this serve as a reminder of God's unwavering favor in your life. Keep your faith strong, find joy in His guidance, and trust in the victory He is leading you toward. Your battles will not be in vain, for His favor is with you every step of the way.

Week 18 Thursday

Laugh With Belief!

"And Sarah said, "God has made me laugh, and all who hear will laugh with me." (Genesis 21:6, NKJV)

In Genesis 18, God made an extraordinary promise to Sarah—that she would bear a son despite being ninety years old and childless. Initially, Sarah laughed in disbelief. It seemed unimaginable that such a miracle could happen, even though God had already declared to Abraham that she would become "a mother of nations" (Genesis 17:16). Her laughter reflected the doubts and limitations of human understanding.

But God's word never fails. When Isaac was born, Sarah's laughter transformed. No longer rooted in disbelief, her laughter became a joyful expression of amazement at God's faithfulness. Holding her long-awaited child in her arms, she and Abraham named him Isaac, which means "laughter," a testament to the power of God to fulfill His promises.

Just as God placed His promise in Sarah's arms, He desires to do the same for us. Some of His promises may feel impossible or difficult to believe, leaving us tempted to laugh in disbelief as Sarah once did. But God calls us to trust Him fully, knowing that His power surpasses all limitations.

It's time to let go of doubt and embrace faith in His ability to accomplish the impossible. Rejoice with laughter, not in disbelief, but in anticipation of what God will do. His promises are unshakable, and His timing is perfect. Trust in Him, for He is the same God who brought laughter to Sarah's heart—and He longs to bring His promises to fulfillment in your life as well!

Week 18 Friday

God Sees Our Potentials!

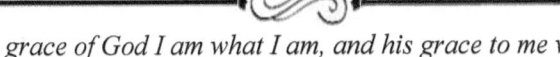

"But by the grace of God I am what I am, and his grace to me was not without effect." (1 Corinthians 15:10, NIV)

The person God created us to be can often feel overshadowed by the influences of the world—compromise, impatience, envy, and jealousy can creep in and hold us back from living fully in His purpose. Yet, what remains constant is God's unwavering love and faithfulness. He never gives up on us. No matter how far we stray or how many mistakes we make, He continues to call us back to Him, gently guiding us toward the path He has lovingly designed for our lives.

Much like a parent's love for their child, God's love is steadfast. He sees the immense potential within us, even when we feel unworthy or inadequate. He doesn't just wait for us to succeed—He actively supports us, offering His favor, blessings, and even unexpected opportunities to help us grow and thrive. Time and again, He exceeds our wildest expectations, proving His faithfulness in ways that leave us in awe.

God is also a master at removing obstacles from our lives. Whether we're facing challenges or enduring setbacks, He has the power to clear the way, making room for His purpose to unfold.

It's important to remember that the Creator of the universe is not distant or unreachable. He is our Heavenly Father, full of love and compassion, always ready to meet us where we are. No matter where you are in your journey, take heart—He is walking alongside you, helping you become the person He intended you to be. Trust in His love and let Him lead you forward.

Week 19 Monday

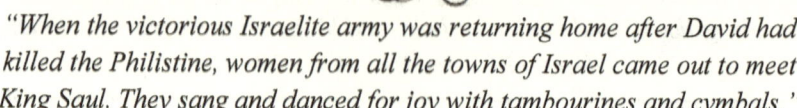
Problems Are Promotions!

"When the victorious Israelite army was returning home after David had killed the Philistine, women from all the towns of Israel came out to meet King Saul. They sang and danced for joy with tambourines and cymbals."
(1 Samuel 18:6, NLT)

We must regularly remind ourselves that challenges are a natural part of life, and at times, we will face unfair treatment from others. Throughout our journey, there will be situations that impact us emotionally and mentally, leaving us feeling drained or disheartened. It's normal to feel discouraged and even lose motivation in the face of adversity. However, God has an incredible way of turning our difficulties into something meaningful when there is purpose behind them.

God doesn't send the challenges, but He is masterful at using them to our advantage. Every obstacle we face holds the potential to be an opportunity for growth. What may feel like a setback can actually be a setup for God to bring about something new and better in our lives. In these moments, it's important to shift our perspective and trust in His greater plan.

Though it may be hard to rejoice during life's storms, perseverance is key. Worrying will never change our circumstances, but praise and worship have the power to uplift our hearts and strengthen our spirits.

Take comfort in knowing that God walks beside you through every trial, working behind the scenes for your good. Keep your faith alive, and trust that He is turning your struggles into stepping stones for something greater. Your breakthrough is closer than you think.

Week 19 Tuesday

God Holds Our Destiny!

"In him we were also chosen, having been predestined according to the plan of him who works out everything in conformity with the purpose of his will." (Ephesians 1:11, NIV)

We are blessed with the gift of free will, enabling us to make decisions and choose our paths. The choices we make shape the course of our lives, leading us down roads of our own design. Yet, God has a plan and purpose for each of us—a future filled with hope, joy, and fulfillment. His plan for our lives exists beyond and independent of our choices, demonstrating His unwavering love and grace.

Even when we make wrong turns or poor decisions, God's purpose for us remains steadfast. Though our missteps may divert us, He continually works to draw us back to His path. When we come before Him, surrendering our hearts and inviting His guidance, He lovingly realigns us. God not only redeems what was lost, but He also propels us into the future He intended, restoring what may feel impossible to recover.

This is the beauty of God's grace—His willingness to meet us where we are and guide us to where we're meant to be. His love for us is greater than our mistakes, and His desire is for us to live in alignment with His divine plan.

Today, choose to trust in Him and align your life with His purpose. Let go of worry about past choices, and allow God to take the lead. As you follow His guidance, you'll experience the joy, peace, and fulfillment He has lovingly prepared for you. His plans are always worth embracing.

Week 19 Wednesday

Focus on Happiness

"Do not be anxious about anything, but in every situation, by prayer and petition, with thanksgiving, present your requests to God. And the peace of God, which transcends all understanding, will guard your hearts and your minds in Christ Jesus." (Philippians 4:6–7, NIV)

The scripture encourages us, *"Do not be anxious about anything,"* a gentle reminder that life will always have its share of challenges. No one is exempt—regardless of age, background, or situation. These difficulties aren't a reflection of weak faith but rather a reality of life's unpredictability and the trials the enemy places in our path.

To navigate these challenges, our minds need reconditioning. We must learn to accept life's realities while refusing to let worry take control. It's essential to direct our thoughts intentionally, allowing our minds to work *for* us rather than against us. Instead of dwelling on problems and allowing anxiety to overwhelm us, we can choose to shift our focus toward joy, gratitude, and the blessings in our lives.

When stress arises, let it become an opportunity for prayer. Turn your worries into conversations with God, presenting your concerns with a heart of thankfulness. Gratitude changes perspective, opening our eyes to God's goodness even in the midst of trials.

Reframe your challenges as opportunities to grow closer to God, to trust Him more deeply, and to experience His love anew. Let gratitude and prayer be your anchors, allowing His peace to steady your heart. No matter what you face, remember He is faithful and working in every detail of your life. With His presence guiding you, joy will always outshine worry. You've got this!

Week 19 Thursday

Hope For It!

"Now faith is the substance of things hoped for, the evidence of things not seen." (Hebrews 11:1, NKJV)

Faith, as described in scripture, is the evidence of things not seen. It teaches us that God does not require tangible proof from us to trust Him for the unseen—faith simply asks us to hope and believe. The unseen knows no boundaries; it encompasses the deep beliefs and desires we hold in our hearts, even when there's no visible evidence to support them.

There are moments in life when we're called to believe in something that seems beyond reach, relying solely on God's infinite power and grace. This trust is what defines faith—a confident assurance in God's ability to accomplish the impossible. It challenges us to shift our focus from what is visible to what is yet to come, trusting that His plans far exceed anything we can imagine.

God invites us to approach Him boldly with our requests, never placing limits on what we can ask of Him. He responds in extraordinary ways, showering us with favor, blessings, and unexpected opportunities. He works behind the scenes, aligning us with the right people and circumstances at just the right time, ensuring His promises are fulfilled.

As you pursue the desires of your heart, hold tightly to faith. Even in moments of doubt or uncertainty, remain steadfast, knowing that God is faithful. Keep pressing forward, believing that He is working all things together for your good. With faith as your foundation, there's no limit to what God can do in your life. Trust Him completely and never give up—His blessings are closer than you realize!

Week 19 Friday

Give Yourself More Credit!

"Whoever is slow to anger is better than the mighty, and he who rules his spirit than he who takes a city." (Proverbs 16:32, ESV)

We each carry within us a unique personal space made up of our thoughts, feelings, emotions, attitudes, and behaviors. This space belongs entirely to us, and each component is within our control. While external factors—like past hurts, traumas, abuse, insecurities, lack of confidence, and low self-esteem—can exert pressure and influence our reactions, they don't define us. Recognizing that we are always in the driver's seat of our lives is key to maintaining control over our choices and actions.

Life's pressures can be intense, but it's important to remember that no one can force us into actions we don't truly desire. The decisions we make are ours to own. Scripture reminds us to be slow to anger, teaching us that ruling our spirit is a source of tremendous power. This self-control has the potential to create positive change, even to the extent of taking a city.

Don't underestimate yourself. You have the power to shape your reactions and steer your life in the direction you choose. Give yourself more credit for the resilience and wisdom you already possess. Embracing self-control allows you to rise above challenges and focus on growth and opportunity.

You are the driver of your own journey, equipped to face life's pressures with grace and determination. Trust in your ability to rule your spirit and watch as it opens doors to greater victories and triumphs. Celebrate the control you have—it's a gift that sets you apart!

Week 20 Monday

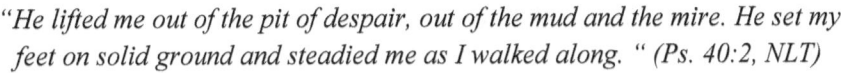
Toxic Soil!

"He lifted me out of the pit of despair, out of the mud and the mire. He set my feet on solid ground and steadied me as I walked along." (Ps. 40:2, NLT)

Have you ever stood near a waste site, where garbage and toxic waste are dumped? Such a place doesn't only affect the people living nearby—it infiltrates the air, water, and soil, spreading contamination. Now, imagine your emotions and thought processes as that soil, absorbing the toxic waste of hurtful words, rejection, betrayals, and the negative actions of others. Just as poison spreads through the environment, so do toxic emotions infiltrate our minds, clouding our future relationships, dreams, behaviors, and attitudes.

None of us are immune to the fumes of these poisonous emotions. They weigh us down, holding us captive in cycles of pain and bitterness. But here's the beautiful truth: we don't have to stay trapped. Forgiveness is the key to freedom. It's a powerful tool that God calls us to use—not just to forgive others as He forgives us, but to forgive ourselves as well.

Forgiveness doesn't mean dismissing the hurt or pretending it didn't happen. Instead, it's a deliberate choice to release the grip of those toxic emotions, freeing your heart to heal and move forward. With God's grace, you can rise above the contamination of life's toxic moments and step into a place of peace and restoration.

Today, choose to let go. Embrace the power of forgiveness, knowing that it's not just for others—it's a gift for yourself. Leave the toxic mud behind, and step boldly into the life God has designed for you, full of hope, healing, and endless possibilities. You deserve to be free.

Week 20 Tuesday

God Believes In You!

"The LORD told Gideon, "With these 300 men I will rescue you and give you victory over the Midianites. Send all the others home." (Judges 7:7, NLT)

Gideon, leading 300 men to face 135,000 Midianite soldiers, was stepping into what seemed like an impossible mission. Some may have questioned whether he was truly following God's guidance or simply misled by doubts or even the enemy. Yet, God saw something in Gideon that defied human reasoning—He called him a "mighty hero." This powerful declaration wasn't based on Gideon's skills, resources, or confidence but on God's unwavering belief in his potential.

This story is a beautiful reflection of how God sees us. Even when we feel unqualified, unsupported, or inexperienced, God looks beyond our limitations and sees the greatness within us. He calls us heroes, capable of overcoming challenges and stepping into victories we can hardly imagine. God isn't limited by what we lack—He works through our faith and obedience to accomplish the extraordinary.

When faced with what seems impossible, it's easy to let doubts and fears take over. But remember, if God has given the green light, His guidance and approval are more powerful than any obstacle or limitation. He equips us to rise above the odds and empowers us to accomplish the unimaginable.

Trust God's plans for your life, and approach each challenge with confidence, knowing that His purpose and favor go before you. He sees your potential even when you don't—and with Him, all things are possible. Embrace the task, and let God show you just how mighty you are in His hands.

Week 20 Wednesday

Hearing God Speaks!

"And He said to them, "He who has ears to hear, let him hear!"
(Mark 4:9, NKJV)

Jesus made this profound statement because He understood how challenging it can be for us to truly hear God's voice. Often, we may confuse our own inner thoughts with His guidance, especially when what we hear doesn't seem to align with our desires or doesn't yet manifest in our lives. When God speaks, His words lead to a manifestation, but they may require patience. His consistency is unwavering—He speaks to us through scripture, people, nature, the still small voice, and other remarkable ways.

Yet, we risk overlooking His message when our focus is solely on hearing what we want to hear. Jesus emphasized the importance of attentive listening throughout the Gospels, repeating the phrase *"He who has ears to hear, let him hear!"* six times. This call to hear deeply extends to Revelation, where He challenges us to listen *"to what the Spirit is saying,"* encouraging us to tune our inner ears to His voice.

It requires us to quiet our minds, calm our spirits, and be intentional about seeking Him. It's in this stillness that we can perceive His guidance and recognize the clarity of His message. God is always speaking—our role is to listen with open hearts.

Today, take a moment to pause and reflect. Make space for stillness, and ask God to reveal what He may be saying to you. His voice is closer than you think, waiting to guide you toward His purpose and peace. Let His presence fill your heart and lead you forward.

Week 20 Thursday

Let God Be God!

"Trust in the LORD with all your heart, and lean not on your own understanding; in all your ways acknowledge Him, and He shall direct your paths." (Proverbs 3:5–6, NKJV)

Believing in God requires faith, especially when we're trusting Him for the things we cannot see. Reflecting on raising seven children with a $22,000 yearly income, a $1,700 monthly mortgage, plus utilities, food, and countless other expenses, it still feels overwhelming to comprehend. How did Kathleen and I manage? The answer lies in faith and reliance on God.

Today, many people wait for financial stability, a home, a car, and a secure job before even considering starting a family. While there's wisdom in being prepared, it's also important to remember that this mindset can sometimes limit the opportunity to let God show His provision and greatness. Everything we have in life is temporary. Finances, material possessions, even our very lives—none of it is guaranteed.

When we put our trust in the Lord with all our hearts, we open ourselves to His blessings and favor. He has a way of providing in unexpected, miraculous ways when we rely on Him fully. Trusting Him doesn't mean life will be without challenges, but it does mean we'll experience His presence, guidance, and provision in ways beyond our expectations.

So, take that leap of faith, whether it's in your family, your dreams, or simply enjoying the blessings of today. Trust wholeheartedly in the Lord, and let Him show you just how faithful He is. His favor is limitless!

Week 20 Friday

We Come Out Victorious!

"Children, you belong to God, and you have defeated these enemies. God's Spirit is in you and is more powerful than the one who is in the world."
(1 John 4:4, CEV)

Some of us may be facing overwhelming situations right now, moments where uncertainty and fear seem to take hold. It's natural to feel stuck, unsure of how things will work out. But the Bible reminds us of a powerful truth—anything that comes against us has already been defeated. The ultimate victory over every challenge and hardship was secured when Jesus died and rose again.

We carry within us God's spirit—the same spirit that raised Jesus from the dead and was present at the very beginning of creation. This truth means we are never without strength, and we have the resilience to stand firm in our battles. The answers we seek, the solutions we need, are already within us because of God's power at work in us.

We must be mindful that the enemy will try to distract us, planting doubt and discouragement in our hearts. But we can stand confidently, knowing that through God, we are equipped for victory. When we fix our hearts on Him, no obstacle can defeat us.

Take heart today and trust in the power of God's spirit within you. Remember that no matter how tough the challenge may seem, you are already victorious. Embrace the confidence that comes from His love and guidance—you were made to overcome and thrive! Keep moving forward with faith and boldness. Victory is already yours.

Week 21 Monday

Don't Act on Impulse!

"She named the child Ichabod (which means "Where is the glory?"), for she said, "Israel's glory is gone." She named him this because the Ark of God had been captured." (1 Samuel 4:21, NLT)

An Israelite woman, about to give birth, received the heartbreaking news that the ark of the covenant—God's tangible presence among the Israelites—had been stolen. Overwhelmed by sorrow and despair, she named her son Ichabod, meaning "the glory has departed." In her anguish, she allowed her disappointment to shape her decision, letting her pain define her child's future by reflecting on her past.

This story reminds us of an important truth: while life's challenges may feel overwhelming, we don't have to let them dictate the way we speak or act. God calls us to choose words and names that carry hope and faith, regardless of our circumstances. He urges us to look forward with expectation, trusting that even in the midst of hardship, He is preparing us for something greater.

The names we speak—whether literal or symbolic—hold power. Rather than letting emotions or adversity lead us to words of despair, we are encouraged to "speak life." Declare God's promises, focus on His faithfulness, and let hope guide your thoughts and actions.

Life's struggles can feel heavy, but they are often setting the stage for remarkable things to come. Don't allow temporary challenges to cloud the vision God has for your life. Speak words of hope, declare faith in His plans, and trust in His goodness. The glory hasn't departed—it's waiting to shine in your future. Keep speaking life!

Week 21 Tuesday

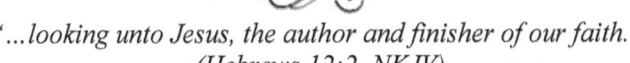

"...looking unto Jesus, the author and finisher of our faith."
(Hebrews 12:2, NKJV)

We are reminded to focus on the future by fixing our eyes on Jesus, the pioneer and perfecter of our faith. He is the one who leads and strengthens us on our journey, guiding us toward the destiny He has planned. To move forward, it's vital to reflect on how our current actions align with the future we envision and to make adjustments when needed.

Our failures, mistakes, and poor choices are not the end of the story. Instead, they are valuable life lessons that shape us and propel us closer to our God-given purpose. Rather than being confined by the weight of the past, we have the opportunity to use it as a foundation for building a brighter, more hopeful future.

Jesus is the completer of our faith, the one who holds us together during trials and enables us to achieve remarkable things. With Him, we can approach life with confidence, knowing that His presence empowers us to overcome any obstacle.

When envisioning your future, take time to think about the legacy you want to leave—the stories of resilience, strength, and courage that inspire others. Remember to celebrate your worth and acknowledge the journey you've taken so far. Give yourself credit for your perseverance and trust in God's perfect plan. The future is full of hope, and with Jesus leading the way, there are no limits to what you can achieve!

Week 21 Wednesday

Let God Navigate

"Trust in the LORD with all your heart, and lean not on your own understanding; in all your ways acknowledge Him, and He shall direct your paths.." (Proverbs 3:5–6, NKJV)

This has been a cornerstone of comfort during some of my most challenging moments. Trusting in the LORD with unwavering faith has a remarkable way of dissolving stress and worry. When we choose to rely on God wholeheartedly instead of leaning on our own understanding, we create space for Him to guide and direct our paths with His perfect wisdom.

Surrendering control is not always easy, but it is essential to experiencing God's purpose for our lives. Seeking His direction in every area—our relationships, decisions, and plans—allows us to walk in alignment with His divine will. Acknowledging Him in all our ways means inviting an ongoing awareness of His presence, a daily commitment to keep Him at the center of every choice we make.

When we allow God to take the lead in our journey, He brings clarity where there was confusion, purpose where there was uncertainty, and a deep sense of fulfillment as we move forward. His guidance is always steady and sure, even when we face obstacles.

Take time to invite God into your journey today. Release the need to figure it all out on your own, and trust that He is navigating your path with care and love. By leaning on Him, you'll find peace and assurance that surpasses human understanding, propelling you forward with confidence and hope. Let God's hand lead you into the extraordinary plans He has prepared.

Week 21 Thursday

God Blesses!

"God blesses those who patiently endure testing and temptation. Afterward they will receive the crown of life that God has promised to those who love him." (James 1:12, NLT)

Life is filled with challenges—whether in marriages, relationships, finances, parenting, work, or dealing with those who seek to take advantage of us. It's important to remind ourselves that there is no such thing as a perfect, peaceful life without hardships. Problems and struggles will always arise, but how we choose to respond can make all the difference.

In difficult situations, we may feel tested or under immense pressure to act in ways that stray from godliness. It's during these times that remaining faithful and grounded in God's teachings becomes crucial. Rather than succumbing to temptation, we are called to trust Him and seek His guidance. By doing so, we not only honor God but also open the door for Him to work in our lives.

Every challenge presents an opportunity to find the silver lining and transform disadvantages into stepping stones toward growth. Enduring trials with patience and faith allows us to experience God's promises in full. He assures us that blessings will follow when we remain steadfast.

When you see others who seem blessed and favored by God, take a moment to reflect. Their journey likely included trials and temptations that they overcame by trusting in God's plan. Let this encourage you to persevere with the same strength and faith. Remind yourself, "They endured the test and temptation, and so will I." Stay faithful and trust that God's blessings are on their way.

Week 21 Friday

Bless and Multiply!

"When they had all had enough to eat, he said to his disciples, "Gather the pieces that are left over. Let nothing be wasted."(John 6:12, NIV)

Think about the remarkable story of Jesus feeding over five thousand men, not counting women and children, with just five loaves and two fish. He blessed the little that was available and multiplied it into an abundance. This miracle serves as a reminder that even when we feel stuck or believe time has been wasted, God can bring forth abundance from what seems like nothing.

God does not want any part of our lives to go to waste. Just as Jesus multiplied the small amount of food, God desires to take what we have—no matter how little it may seem—and turn it into more than enough. His blessings aren't limited to physical needs; they extend to wisdom, guidance, and the support we need to make good choices and fulfill His purpose for our lives.

When we trust Him, God can transform even the smallest resources, opportunities, or moments into something significant. He doesn't just bless us for today but also for our families and the generations to come.

If you're feeling discouraged or like you don't have enough, trust in God's ability to multiply what you have. Let His provision fill your heart with hope and confidence, knowing that He is always at work, creating abundance from the little we place in His hands. With God, there's always more than enough for the road ahead.

Week 22 Monday

Don't Lose Hope!

"I am the LORD; when the time is right, I will do this swiftly."
(Isaiah 60:22, ISV)

We all carry dreams and goals close to our hearts—whether it's finding the right job, pursuing the proper education, discovering the perfect relationship, achieving financial stability, or no longer living pay cheque to pay cheque. Many of us hope to see improvements in our mental and physical health as well. Yet, the waiting period can often feel difficult and discouraging, leaving us frustrated and longing for answers.

It's important to remember that everything unfolds in God's perfect timing. He knows when we are ready to receive what we've been asking for and guides us toward the destiny He has lovingly prepared. The scripture reassures us, *"I am the LORD; when the time is right, I will do this swiftly."* God's timing is never late, and His plans for us are full of purpose and hope.

Believe with confidence that when the right moment comes, everything will align, and God will swiftly move you toward your future. He has the power to bring your dreams into reality, often in ways far greater than you could imagine. Trust in Him through the waiting season, knowing that He is working behind the scenes for your good.

Rather than letting the waiting period weigh you down, choose to enjoy the journey. Embrace each moment with hope and gratitude, trusting that God's hand is guiding your steps. Your breakthrough is coming, and His plans for your life are always worth the wait!

Week 22 Tuesday
Don't Run Away!

"When the sailors heard this, they were frightened because Jonah had already told them he was running from the LORD." (Jonah 1:10, CEV)

Many of us, like Jonah, have moments when we want to run away from challenges or demanding situations. Jonah chose to flee from his task, and similarly, we may avoid facing those who have wronged us, bypassing the path of forgiveness. This can hinder the freeing of our minds from the weight of negativity. By not addressing our hurt feelings directly, we may unintentionally magnify them, trapping ourselves in cycles of bitterness and resentment.

Avoidance, whether of life's hurdles or unresolved pain, blocks the manifestation of true love and prevents us from fully experiencing God's greatness. My own journey involved 26 years of carrying emotional pain. I avoided facing it and withheld forgiveness—from myself and the person involved. However, when I finally addressed it, I experienced a profound sense of liberation, as if a heavy burden had been lifted. It was a reminder of the freedom that forgiveness brings.

We are called to rise above avoidance and confront life with courage and faith. By embracing the challenges before us, we can respond fully to God's call on our lives. Each step of reconciliation, forgiveness, and endurance leads us closer to His purpose and fills us with His love.

Don't let fear or avoidance hold you back. Trust in God's guidance and allow Him to work in your heart, freeing you to live life to the fullest. There's freedom and purpose on the other side of every challenge. Respond to His call!

Week 22 Wednesday

Sprinkle The Sweetness

"Kind words are like honey—sweet to the soul and healthy for the body."
(Proverbs 16:24, NLT)

Scripture beautifully reminds us that kind words are like honey—sweet to the soul and healing to the body. This wisdom holds deep meaning in our everyday interactions and relationships. Offering kindness to our spouse nurtures love and strengthens the foundation of a marriage, creating a bond that weathers life's challenges. Sharing kind words with our children builds trust and fosters emotional security, providing them with a sense of belonging and care. Similarly, showing kindness to parents honours the family connection, deepening the love that ties generations together.

Kindness extends beyond our families. To friends and colleagues, kind words foster encouragement, support, and positivity, creating an environment where everyone can thrive. Through small, intentional acts of kindness, we can transform our communities into havens of warmth and compassion.

Let us sprinkle kindness across all areas of our lives, recognizing its power to create a healthier, more harmonious existence for ourselves and those we care about. By choosing kindness, we leave a legacy of love and hope, enriching the lives of everyone we encounter.

Take a moment today to speak kind words to those around you. A simple act of kindness can ripple through hearts, fostering love, healing, and connection in ways you may never fully realize. Let kindness be your gift to the world.

Week 22 Thursday

Reduce Tension

"You make known to me the path of life; you will fill me with joy in your presence, with eternal pleasures at your right hand." (Psalm 16:11, NIV)

God's light illuminates the path of life, and His presence fills us with unshakable joy. At His right hand, we are gifted with eternal pleasures—a privilege that reminds us of His unwavering love and guidance. It's important to resist the urge to defer happiness, waiting for everything in life to align perfectly. Each day is a precious gift, brimming with moments to cherish and opportunities to embrace.

When life feels uncertain or challenging, find solace in knowing that God is your source of strength and help. Unfold life's imperfections with grace, trusting that He is working all things together for your good. Let go of tension, manage your stress, and avoid the cycle of questioning when answers seem elusive. Instead, nurture a steadfast faith, believing that God is in control and leading you toward your destined purpose.

Remember that challenges do not have the power to hold you back. God's presence melts away the darkness, clearing the way for His joy to shine brightly in your heart. Let that joy arise—it is a gift that brings peace and renewal, enabling you to face life's hurdles with confidence and hope.

Today, embrace the fullness of joy and trust in God's plan for your life. Allow His light to guide you forward, and let the peace of His presence reduce the burdens that weigh on your spirit. Joy is within you, ready to uplift and restore—let it take root and flourish!

Week 22 Friday

You Will Be Favoured!

"The LORD caused the Egyptians to look favorably on the Israelites, and they gave the Israelites whatever they asked for. So they stripped the Egyptians of their wealth!" (Exodus 12:36, NLT)

When God liberated the Israelites from 430 years of Egyptian slavery, He didn't just grant them freedom—He showered them with favor and blessings. The Egyptians, despite being their oppressors, were compelled to give them silver, gold, and clothing. God turned their years of suffering into a season of abundance, paying them back for the mistreatment they had endured. He transformed their story from one of hardship to one filled with joy, gifts, and restoration.

This incredible story serves as a reminder that, even in our most challenging seasons, we can trust that God is working to bring justice to our lives. He sees every struggle, every disappointment, and every moment of lack. And just as He did for the Israelites, God desires to turn the tables for us too. His plan for our lives is not one of burden or sickness, but one of blessings, abundance, and health.

Take heart in knowing that God is a God of restoration. He reclaims what has been stolen—whether it's joy, peace, health, finances, relationships, or dreams—and breathes new life into it.

Be at peace today, knowing that God is faithful to His promises. Release your worries, and let Him carry the weight of your burdens. Trust in His ability to rectify every wrong and to transform your struggles into blessings. With God, restoration is always near. Let Him renew your spirit and guide you into a future filled with hope and abundance.

Week 23 Monday

Prioritize God!

"For the LORD your God is bringing you into a good land—a land with brooks, streams, and deep springs gushing out into the valleys and hills." (Deuteronomy 8:7, NIV)

God has a prepared place for each of us, just as He did for His people in scripture. If you find yourself in a space that doesn't reflect the goodness He has planned, don't settle there. To experience the fullness of His blessings, we must follow His way. It's our obedience that unlocks the doors to His promises. By humbling ourselves before Him and persevering with faith and expectancy, we position ourselves to receive all He has prepared.

Let God guide you into the good land He has set aside for you—a place overflowing with abundant resources, favor, health, creativity, meaningful friendships, joy, and peace. This is a space of increase and opportunity, where His provision exceeds expectations. Strive to honor Him with your choices and let obedience pave the way for His blessings to flow into your life.

Prioritize God above all else, allowing His guidance to direct your steps toward the promise of goodness. It begins with surrender—trusting Him, following His lead, and maintaining a heart of humility. Keep moving forward, holding onto faith and positive expectations, knowing that He is walking alongside you and working on your behalf.

Today, embrace His calling and let Him lead you into the fullness of His plans. With God, every step brings you closer to the good land He has promised—a place where His love, provision, and joy abound. You were made for this!

Week 23 Tuesday

A Glad Welcome!

"Now we can come fearlessly right into God's presence, assured of his glad welcome when we come with Christ and trust in him." (Ephesians 3:12, TLB)

God welcomes us with boundless joy every time we approach Him. Just as loving parents or cherished friends eagerly anticipate our visits, He delights in our presence and longs for us to draw near. Unlike earthly relationships that may have limitations, we can boldly come to God at any time and from anywhere, knowing He not only accepts us but treasures our companionship.

The more time we spend with God, the deeper our bond with Him grows. This relationship, much like the closeness we feel with loved ones, transforms into something extraordinary—a profound connection of the soul. It becomes an intimate longing to be in His presence, where peace, love, and security abound.

Let us resolve to make spending quality time with God a priority, nurturing this beautiful relationship that brings joy to both our hearts and His. In moments of prayer, reflection, and worship, we experience His divine embrace, a source of strength and renewal that uplifts every part of our being.

It is in His presence that blessings and favor are poured out abundantly. As we align our hearts with His, we open ourselves to the goodness He desires to share. Today, take a moment to draw close to God, knowing He is eagerly awaiting you with open arms. Let this connection be your anchor, guiding you to the fullness of life He has lovingly prepared for you. God's joy is your sanctuary—embrace it wholeheartedly!

Week 23 Wednesday

Avoid The Distraction

"Dear brothers, is your life full of difficulties and temptations? Then be happy, for when the way is rough, your patience has a chance to grow."
(James 1:2–3, TLB)

As we journey through life, challenges and daily temptations are inevitable. These real-life struggles often test our strength and resilience, but they also present opportunities for growth. In moments of difficulty, we have the ability not only to endure but to rise above and flourish. By acknowledging the tangible aspects of our lives that pose difficulties, we can recognize that every obstacle is an opportunity for perseverance to build strength and character.

Finding joy amid everyday struggles is key. When we trust that God can transform practical obstacles into remarkable opportunities, we unlock the potential to see His power at work in the most tangible areas of our lives. He is capable of turning trials into triumphs, bringing purpose and blessings into places where we once felt stuck.

As you navigate these moments, set meaningful goals and press forward with faith and determination. Remember, you are never alone in this journey—God walks alongside you, with great plans already prepared for your future. Resist the temptation to dwell in sadness or make choices that could lead you away from His path. These distractions only serve to keep you from the extraordinary blessings that lie ahead.

Keep your eyes fixed on what's to come and move forward with confidence. Trust in God's timing and His unwavering guidance, knowing that every step is bringing you closer to the wonderful things He has in store for you. You are made to overcome and flourish!

Week 23 Thursday

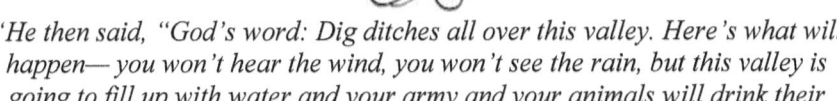

"He then said, "God's word: Dig ditches all over this valley. Here's what will happen— you won't hear the wind, you won't see the rain, but this valley is going to fill up with water and your army and your animals will drink their fill." (2 Kings 3:16–17, MSG)

After journeying through the desert for seven exhausting days, Judah and Israel's armies found themselves parched and desperate. In this moment of need, the prophet Elisha gave them an unexpected directive—to dig ditches in the valley. Though tired, doubtful, and uncertain, they obeyed with fervor. The next day, in a miraculous turn, water flowed into the valley, filling every ditch they had dug. God's provision came in abundance, rewarding their faith and effort.

God's instructions often defy logic, but they carry a purpose far beyond what we can comprehend. It's a reminder that we shouldn't hesitate or settle for minimal effort when following His guidance. Instead, we should go all in—don't just dig small ditches; grab a bulldozer and dig deep and wide. Trusting His direction, even when it feels unconventional or perplexing, opens the door to blessings we never imagined.

This is a call to stir up your faith, especially when life doesn't seem to make sense. Trust that God's ways are higher, and He is always working for your good. Embrace His guidance with a heart willing to act, knowing He will provide abundantly.

Strive to give your very best and then some, trusting that God's plans are far greater than what you can see. When you align your actions with His instructions, you'll witness His extraordinary blessings unfold. Keep digging, and let faith lead the way!

Week 23 Friday
Forget What Happened!

"The God who summons horses and chariots and armies—they lie down and then can't get up; they're snuffed out like so many candles: "Forget about what's happened; don't keep going over old history. Be alert, be present. I'm about to do something brand-new." (Isaiah 43:17–19, MSG)

The powerful image of God dismantling mighty horses, chariots, and armies speaks profoundly to our personal journeys. It serves as a touching reminder to let go of the burdens of our past—the emotional pain, regrets, mistakes, and wrong choices that weigh us down—just as those formidable forces were brought to nothing. These words, *"forget about what's happened,"* carry a deep emotional resonance, calling us to release the scars of old battles and the challenges we've endured.

By choosing to let go and staying fully present, we allow ourselves to open our hearts to the possibility of something entirely new. This act of release isn't just about moving forward; it's about preparing the way for God to do something transformative in our lives. It's an invitation to embrace renewal, to trust in His ability to bring beauty and hope where there once was pain.

This verse intimately connects to our struggles, offering encouragement to anticipate God's touch in even the most complex circumstances. It speaks to the promise of His renewal—a promise that stirs our souls and fills us with optimism. When we lay down the weight of our past, we create space for His light to shine brighter and for His blessings to take root.

Week 24 Monday

Overshadowed By God

"The angel answered, "The Holy Spirit will come on you, and the power of the Most High will overshadow you." (Luke 1:35, NIV)

The angel's message to Mary, delivered through the Holy Spirit, serves as a beautiful reminder of God's constant influence and presence in our lives. It inspires us to remain open to the Holy Spirit's guidance, allowing His transformative power to shape our thoughts, actions, and decisions. When we invite the Holy Spirit into our hearts, we create space for profound change, aligning ourselves with God's purpose and grace.

This sacred encounter encourages us to reflect deeply on spiritual insights and recognize the incredible potential for renewal when we live in harmony with His divine will. Being in the shadow of God means dwelling in His protection and favor, a place where miracles unfold, doors of opportunity open, and breakthroughs occur.

Let this serve as a call to expect God to work powerfully through us. Trust that He orchestrates divine appointments in our lives—moments where His plans for us intersect with His blessings. It is in these moments of faith and surrender that we witness the extraordinary, feeling His hand actively guiding our journey.

Take time today to quiet your heart and be receptive to the Holy Spirit's voice. Embrace His presence, knowing that He is working in and through you to bring about His plans. In God's shadow, there is no limit to what can be achieved. Live with expectation, and let His transformative power unfold in your life. Miracles await!

Week 24 Tuesday

Challenging Understanding

"How will this be," Mary asked the angel, "since I am a virgin?"
(Luke 1:34, NIV)

Mary's question to the angel in Luke 1:34 reflects her profound uncertainty and wonder as she confronts the seemingly impossible news of her divine conception. Her response captures a moment of human vulnerability—a natural reaction to something beyond understanding. This verse serves as a powerful reminder that life often presents us with situations that challenge our reasoning and expectations.

Just as Mary approached her uncertainty with openness, we are encouraged to respond to life's mysteries with faith and trust. There will be times when we face challenges that feel insurmountable, moments when God's plans seem beyond our grasp. Yet, this scripture invites us to lean into His guidance, trusting that He sees the bigger picture and knows what's best for us.

Faith doesn't mean we need to have all the answers—it means surrendering our doubts and embracing humility, allowing God to work in ways that transcend our understanding. Even in the midst of uncertainty, we can hold onto the assurance that His plans are intentional, purposeful, and filled with grace.

Let this verse remind you to expect the unexpected from God. His surprises often come at the most unlikely times, revealing His greatness and faithfulness in ways we couldn't imagine. Whatever uncertainty you may be facing, take heart in knowing that His plans for you are good. Trust Him to lead the way, and be open to the extraordinary things He has prepared!

Week 24 Wednesday

It's Who We Are

"And a voice came from heaven: "You are my Son, whom I love; with you I am well pleased." (Luke 3:22, NIV)

At Jesus's baptism, God proclaimed, *"You are my Son, whom I love; with you I am well pleased."* This declaration was made before Jesus had begun His ministry, performed any miracles, or delivered profound teachings like the Sermon on the Mount. God's pleasure was not based on Jesus's actions or achievements—it was rooted in His identity as God's beloved Son.

This powerful moment highlights an important truth for all of us: our value in God's eyes is not dependent on our accomplishments, talents, or the opinions of others. We are cherished simply because of who we are—His children, created in His image. Just as Jesus's worth was not tied to His future deeds, our worth remains constant in God's eyes, regardless of our successes or failures.

Let this serve as a reminder of God's unwavering love for you. He sees you for who you truly are, not for what you do. His delight in you is unshaken, no matter where you are on your journey. Embrace this truth as a source of comfort and strength, knowing that God's love for you is unconditional and eternal.

Today, remind yourself that you are deeply loved and valued simply for being you. God is pleased with the heart He has shaped within you. Take hold of this truth and carry it with confidence—it is a reflection of His incredible grace and goodness!

Week 24 Thursday

Make Every Moment Counts!

"Make the most of every living and breathing moment because these are evil times." (Ephesians 5:16, VOICE)

This scripture reminds us to seize every living and breathing moment, especially given the challenges of our times. Life often brings unexpected trials, yet within these moments, we find opportunities to rise with resilience and faith. Consider the story of Joseph, who transformed adversity into triumph, or Esther, whose courage changed the course of history. Their examples remind us that even in uncertainty, God's purpose shines through.

Our lives, much like theirs, are shaped by both challenges and the choices we make in response. Ephesians 5:16 calls us to make the most of every moment, turning each day into a chance for growth, acts of kindness, and a deeper relationship with God. By embracing this mindset, we open our hearts to His presence and guidance, even amidst life's difficulties.

Let this verse inspire you to live with intention. Take advantage of life's precious moments and treasure the time you have with the people God has placed in your life. Choose joy, compassion, and faith, knowing that each day holds purpose. Even in the face of life's complexities, God equips us to navigate with grace and hope.

Today is a gift, and tomorrow isn't promised. Embrace the present fully, pouring love into your relationships and pursuing what matters most. With God's wisdom, we can make each moment count, leaving a legacy of faith and gratitude wherever we go. Let your life reflect His light.

Week 24 Friday

God Is On Your Walk!

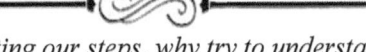

"Since the Lord is directing our steps, why try to understand everything that happens along the way?" (Proverbs 20:24, TLB)

Reflecting on the lives of biblical champions, we discover unexpected twists, delays, and moments of disappointment. These individuals faced distressing setbacks and often felt the weight of life's uncertainties. From Adam and Eve's disobedience to David's grave mistake with Bathsheba, Peter's impulsive denial of Jesus three times, and Saul—later known as Paul—beginning his journey by persecuting Christians, their stories reveal imperfections that resonate with us today.

Yet, despite their flaws and failures, these individuals experienced the redemptive power of God's grace. Their journeys highlight a profound truth: God's mercy endures even in the face of human frailty. He transforms brokenness into beauty, showcasing His unwavering love and ability to redeem our lives. These narratives serve as powerful reminders that no mistake is too great for God to forgive, and no setback is beyond His ability to restore.

God walks beside you through every challenge, offering His mercy and grace to guide you forward. Even in moments of doubt or missteps, His love remains steadfast, ready to bring transformation and hope.

Let the stories of these champions inspire you to trust in God's plan for your life. He can take your imperfections and turn them into a testimony of His greatness. Be encouraged, knowing that God is with you, shaping your path and leading you toward His promises. You are never alone!

Week 25 Monday

The Power in Serving!

"...whoever wants to become great among you must be your servant...just as the Son of Man did not come to be served, but to serve, and to give his life as a ransom for many." (Matthew 20:26–28, NIV)

As believers, we are called to follow the ultimate example set by Christ. Jesus embodied love, care, and humility, reminding us of the beauty in putting others before ourselves. One of the most powerful examples of His servant heart was when He washed His disciples' feet—a profound act of love and humility. It wasn't about the action itself; it was about serving selflessly, with no expectation of anything in return.

When we serve with this same heart, it goes far beyond merely completing tasks. It's about truly understanding others, offering kindness, and fostering genuine connections. Serving with compassion transforms not just those around us but also our own hearts, allowing us to grow and reflect the character of Christ.

Carrying His nature means embracing love, humility, and selflessness in everything we do. It's a reminder that, as His children, we are called to shine His light through our actions. Every act of service, no matter how small, brings a sense of purpose and joy—a reward that comes from aligning our hearts with His.

Take a moment today to perform an act of service, whether it's a kind word, a helping hand, or simply being present for someone in need. By serving others, you mirror Christ's love and create a ripple of kindness that touches lives. Embrace the joy of serving, and let His light shine through you!

Week 25 Tuesday

Double Portion Of Goodness!

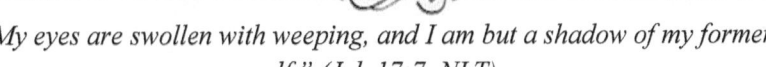

"My eyes are swollen with weeping, and I am but a shadow of my former self." (Job 17:7, NLT)

Job endured sudden, life-altering challenges, losing his loved ones, possessions, and grappling with severe illness. Despite his unwavering faith and devotion to God, he found himself in a profound trial that tested the core of his spirit. Like Job, we may sometimes feel like a shadow of our former selves—once strong and thriving, but now weakened by illness, loss, or hardships that weigh heavily on our lives.

Yet, Job's story did not end in despair, and neither will yours. God orchestrated a remarkable turnaround for Job, restoring his fortunes and doubling his blessings. This powerful reminder shows us that the hardships we endure are not the end of our journey. God's plans are far greater than the struggles we face.

After seasons of pain and loss, you can trust that God is working behind the scenes to bring forth health, happiness, and favour that surpasses what you've experienced before. The difficulties you face today are not your final destination. Instead, they are part of a path that leads to greater abundance and joy.

Take heart and hold onto faith during tough times. Like Job, your story is one of resilience, restoration, and divine favor. God's promise of a double portion of goodness awaits you—a season filled with renewal and blessings beyond imagination. Trust Him to transform your trials into triumphs and lead you into a brighter, richer future.

Week 25 Wednesday

Our Life Line!

"The Lord will fight for you, and you shall hold your peace and remain at rest." (Exodus 14:14, AMPC).

In times when we face personal attacks or feel the sting of hurtful words, it's essential to remember that God is our ultimate defender. Life often presents moments where the actions or words of others leave us feeling wounded and vulnerable, cutting deeply into our hearts and minds. While we may not have control over the wrongdoing of others or the negativity directed at us, we can find refuge and strength in God's promise to stand by us.

Scripture offers us a lifeline—a reminder that we are never alone in these battles. Placing our trust in God as our defender helps us release the need to retaliate or carry the burden of those wounds. His protective presence empowers us to rise above the pain, transforming our struggles into opportunities for growth.

This trust in God acts as a coping mechanism, nurturing a wellspring of inner resilience and peace. It enables us to shift our focus from the hurt to the healing, from the attacks of others to the love and care of our Creator. By anchoring ourselves in His unwavering support, we are reminded of our worth and His ability to bring justice in His time.

Let God's defense be your shield. With His strength, you can flourish even in the face of adversity, walking forward with confidence, grace, and an unshakable peace that comes from His love and protection.

Week 25 Thursday

The Battle Is The Lord's!

"All those gathered here will know that it is not by sword or spear that the LORD saves; for the battle is the LORD's, and he will give all of you into our hands." (1 Samuel 17:47 NIV)

Consider the story of David bravely facing Goliath. With unwavering faith, he declared, *"It's not about swords or spears; the LORD is taking care of this battle."* In the same way, we can find peace in knowing that God stands with us through life's trials, ready to lead us toward victory. Rather than allowing worries to consume us, we are invited to place our trust in Him and watch as His presence makes our challenges fade away.

This trust in God becomes our anchor, grounding us as we navigate tough times with confidence and strength. It's the assurance that the significant victories in our lives are securely held in His hands. Just as David stepped forward with courage, relying on God's power rather than his own, we, too, can face life's giants knowing that God's plan is greater than any obstacle.

Let's carry this sense of trust and confidence wherever we go, knowing that with God on our side, there is nothing we cannot overcome. Instead of allowing stress or fear to cloud our hearts, let's rest in the promise that when He steps in, our problems scatter. This profound trust not only sustains us through challenges but also equips us to move forward with hope and clarity, knowing that every victory is in His capable hands. With faith, we can face the impossible and rise stronger than before!

Week 25 Friday

The Same

"Jesus Christ is the same yesterday and today and forever"
(Hebrews 13:8, NIV).

In the midst of life's uncertainties, find peace in the unwavering nature of our Saviour. Scripture reminds us, *"Jesus Christ is the same yesterday and today and forever"* (Hebrews 13:8, NIV). His enduring love and faithfulness are a source of constant hope, offering us strength as we navigate life's challenges.

The Bible beautifully captures Jesus's unchanging compassion—from His encounter with the woman at the well, offering her grace and acceptance, to His healing touch that restored the leper's life. Just as He walked the shores of Galilee, extending mercy and love, His character remains steadfast, serving as a rock in the midst of our storms.

This timeless truth assures us that the same Saviour who calmed the seas, healed the sick, and conquered death is by our side today. His presence offers the peace we seek, reminding us that we are never alone, no matter the uncertainties or trials we face.

Let the constancy of His love inspire confidence in your heart. In every season of life, whether marked by joy or difficulty, Jesus stands as our wellspring of hope and redemption. He is a reminder that even amid turmoil, His grace and strength are unchanging, a foundation upon which we can always depend.

Embrace the assurance of His steadfast love today. Allow His presence to guide and uplift you, knowing that His promises endure forever. With Jesus, there is always hope.

Week 26 Monday

Align To God's Timeline

"In the morning, LORD, you hear my voice; in the morning, I lay my requests before you and wait expectantly." (Psalm 5:3, NIV)

Waiting for solutions when we feel stuck in life can be one of the hardest challenges we face. We long for answers to appear quickly, and when clarity doesn't come, negative thoughts can creep into our minds. Yet, even in these moments, we can find peace in trusting that God's timing is always perfect. He is never too late and holds a far greater plan for us than we could ever imagine. While we see only the present, God sees tomorrow, and His perspective transcends what we can grasp.

We must resist the urge to confine God to our own timeline. Instead, let us cultivate the faith to wait expectantly after bringing our requests to Him. Trust that He is working behind the scenes, orchestrating a purpose beyond what we can see. No matter what our needs are—whether they are physical, emotional, or spiritual—God's timing is flawlessly aligned with His plan for us.

Believing in a God we cannot see requires faith. But if we truly know that the Creator of the universe is all-powerful and capable, we can offer Him our full trust. When you place 100% of your faith in Him, you'll discover the beauty of relying on His unseen but always-present guidance.

Today, choose to trust in God's perfect timing. Let your heart rest in the assurance that solutions will come, and when they do, they will be far greater than you ever imagined. Faith brings peace, even in the waiting.

Week 26 Tuesday

God Rewards Faithfulness!

"And because the gracious hand of my God was on me, the king granted my requests." (Nehemiah 2:8, NIV)

Nehemiah served faithfully as a devoted cupbearer in the Persian court, demonstrating remarkable loyalty in his duties. In a life-changing moment, he felt a divine call to take on the monumental task of rebuilding the walls of Jerusalem. When he approached the Persian King with his heartfelt plea, the King's surprising and compassionate response, *"How can I assist you?"* showed the power of favor. Nehemiah's steadfast faith and loyalty opened the door to divine connections that ultimately led to success.

This story reminds us that faithfulness brings blessings beyond our imagination. When we remain committed and resilient, even in the face of challenges or delayed answers, God sees and rewards our unwavering devotion. Through our persistence and trust, we attract favor and form connections with those who can guide or support us in fulfilling our purpose.

Nehemiah's journey also teaches us the importance of serving others selflessly. By focusing on what we can give rather than what we can gain, we reflect Christ's love in our actions. Serving those God places in our lives is a beautiful expression of humility and devotion that brings joy to both the giver and receiver.

Take inspiration from Nehemiah today. Trust that God's plan is unfolding perfectly, even if the answers seem far off. Keep giving with an open heart, knowing that your faithfulness will not go unnoticed—and the rewards of serving will be richer than you ever imagined.

Week 26 Wednesday

A Thankful Heart!

"Enter his gates with thanksgiving and his courts with praise; give thanks to him and praise his name." (Psalm 100:4, NIV)

One powerful concept often explored in therapy is the idea of a gratitude jar—a practice of reflecting on the blessings in our lives to nurture a thankful mindset. Taking time to acknowledge the gifts surrounding us can transform our perspective and fill our hearts with appreciation.

We can be thankful for the gift of life itself, for the relationships that bring joy and meaning to our days, and for the opportunities that shape and refine us. The lessons we learn through challenges and the moments of happiness that brighten our paths are also sources of gratitude. It extends even to the simplest pleasures—a kind word, the beauty of nature, or a quiet moment of peace. Even life's challenges are opportunities for resilience and growth, allowing us to see the strength we didn't know we had.

Gratitude helps us embrace the beauty woven into our everyday existence. Every heartbeat, every connection, and every experience becomes a reminder of the abundant blessings we've received. It's an invitation to enter God's gates with thanksgiving and His courts with praise, celebrating His goodness in all things.

Today, reflect on the blessings in your life—big or small—and let gratitude fill your heart. Consider adding your thoughts to your own "gratitude jar" to remind yourself of all the goodness that surrounds you. May your day be filled with thankfulness, joy, and a renewed sense of appreciation for the richness of life. Have a truly thankful day!

Week 26 Thursday
He Place Treasures In Us!

"Therefore, if anyone cleanses himself from what is dishonorable, he will be a vessel for honorable use, set apart as holy, useful to the master of the house, ready for every good work." (2 Timothy 2:21, ESV)

We are all called to be vessels of honour, chosen by God to fulfill a unique and meaningful purpose. As His vessels, we are entrusted with carrying out His divine plan—spreading love, compassion, and wisdom to those around us. God has placed treasures within each of us, precious gifts that reflect His glory and intention for our lives.

These treasures are not meant to remain hidden but to be shared, making a positive impact on the world. To do this, we must align ourselves with God's will, allowing His purpose to flow through us. Our lives hold a higher calling beyond merely going through the motions of each day. We are imbued with valuable qualities—love, empathy, wisdom, and the ability to uplift and inspire others.

By embracing our role as God's vessels, we can bring about positive change, foster understanding, and contribute to the well-being of others. It is through this selfless service that we honour our Creator and reflect the divine love He has poured into us.

Take a moment today to remember the treasures you carry as a child of God. Let His light shine through you as you act with kindness, extend compassion, and share wisdom. You were created with purpose, and the gifts within you are designed to bless the world. Step into this calling with confidence and faith, knowing that God is working through you to make a difference.

Week 26 Friday

Be Present!

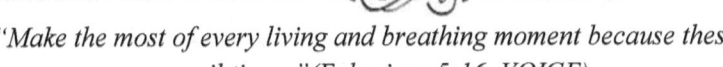

"Make the most of every living and breathing moment because these are evil times." (Ephesians 5:16, VOICE)

To experience true fulfillment, it is essential to embrace a biblical perspective that emphasizes being fully present in life. The wisdom found in scripture encourages us to show up for life with mindfulness, avoiding excessive preoccupation with the past or being overly fixated on the future. While setting goals and envisioning what lies ahead is valuable, it's important not to let such ambitions overshadow the blessings of the present moment.

The Bible gently reminds us of the significance of living in the present. It highlights the profound regret some have felt after neglecting cherished moments with their family, spouse, loved ones, and friends. These relationships are gifts that deserve our attention and care today, not someday. A mindful approach allows us to treasure these connections and appreciate the joys of life's current blessings.

Being present is an act of faith and gratitude—recognizing that each moment is part of God's divine plan and a testament to His goodness. It teaches us to trust in His timing and savor the beauty woven into our daily lives. By aligning ourselves with this biblical perspective, we nurture deeper connections, foster joy in our relationships, and gain a richer understanding of life's purpose.

Take time today to be fully present. Engage with those you love, appreciate the blessings surrounding you, and find peace in the here and now. Fulfillment comes not from chasing tomorrow but from embracing today with an open heart and unwavering faith.

Week 27 Monday

Make Your Faith Impactful!

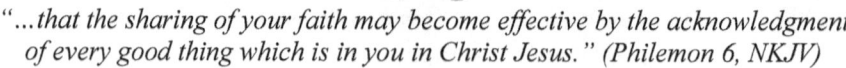

"...that the sharing of your faith may become effective by the acknowledgment of every good thing which is in you in Christ Jesus." (Philemon 6, NKJV)

It's essential to hold onto the truth that every good thing we have comes from the Lord. He is the source of all blessings, and through Christ Jesus, we are richly equipped with gifts that reflect His love and grace. To make our faith truly impactful, we must take time to recognize and celebrate every blessing within us—acknowledging the work Christ has done in our lives.

Instead of focusing on shortcomings or failures, embrace the unique qualities God has bestowed upon you. These attributes are not only gifts but a testament to His handiwork in your life. Allow them to shine brightly, inspiring others and glorifying Him. Be your own encourager, knowing that God has infused His life within you, making you a vessel of His goodness and purpose.

Through His empowerment, you are capable of far more than you can imagine. Faith becomes the key that unlocks opportunities, guiding you to places you never thought possible. As you step forward in trust, God will pour His favor and blessings upon you, preparing the way for greater things.

Today, remind yourself of the treasures God has placed within you. Celebrate His love, embrace the potential He has given, and step boldly into the future He has prepared. With faith, His favor will follow, and His blessings will overflow in your life! Let His goodness shine through you as a reflection of His glory.

Week 27 Tuesday

God's Masterpiece!

"For we are God's masterpiece. He has created us anew in Christ Jesus, so we can do the good things he planned for us long ago." (Ephesians 2:10, NLT)

Our sense of self-worth often stems from how the important people in our lives—like parents, partners, friends, or mentors—perceive us. While these relationships deeply shape us, there will inevitably be moments when someone says or does something hurtful, leaving us feeling less valued. When we base our entire sense of worth on people who, though significant, are still human and imperfect, it's easy to feel insecure or less than enough over time.

To truly embrace our value, we must make God the most important influence in our lives. His love and perspective are unwavering, offering us acceptance, forgiveness, approval, and a profound sense of security. By leaning into what God says about us, we can see ourselves as He does—cherished, capable, and uniquely created.

You are not average or ordinary. God has crafted you with purpose, instilling within you gifts and qualities that reflect His image. Recognizing this divine truth is essential for cultivating a positive and enduring sense of self-worth. It's not the opinions of others but God's unchanging love that defines your true value.

Today, take a moment to remind yourself of this beautiful truth: you are God's masterpiece. Carry this affirmation in your heart and let it guide you to live confidently, knowing you are deeply loved and purposefully created. Your worth is not fleeting—it is grounded in the eternal love of the One who made you. You are extraordinary!

Week 27 Wednesday

He Will Hide You!

"Saul hunted him day after day, but God didn't let Saul find him."
(1 Samuel 23:14, NLT)

There was a time when David fled from King Saul in the Desert of Ziph. Saul's jealousy consumed him, and he became obsessed with taking David's life, despite the fact that David had only ever done good to him. Forced to hide in caves, David found himself pursued by Saul's soldiers, outnumbered and in constant danger. Yet, through it all, God was on David's side. The Bible tells us, *"God didn't let Saul find him."*

This story is a powerful reminder for us today. There may be people in your life who feel threatened by the favor and blessings God has placed upon you. Their envy or resentment may lead them to speak against you or attempt to diminish your value. But take heart—just as God protected David, He will also protect you. He will shield you from unseen dangers, unnecessary distractions, and those who seek to hinder His plans for your life.

Stay faithful and focused on God's purpose for you. Do not allow bitterness or strife to take root in your heart. Instead, trust in the Lord's protection and guidance, knowing that He is working all things together for your good. God's hand over your life is stronger than any obstacle you may face. He will guide you through every trial and keep you on the path to your destiny. Rest in the assurance of His protection and favor, and keep moving forward with faith and confidence.

Week 27 Thursday

Chose Your Battles!

"Take control of what I say, O LORD, and guard my lips."
(Psalm 141:3, NLT)

While delivering food to his brothers, David overheard Goliath taunting the army of Israel. Deeply upset, he began asking the soldiers about the reward for defeating the giant. David wasn't intimidated by Goliath's size but was instead troubled by his insults toward God's people. In that moment, David's older brother, Eliab, overheard him and tried to embarrass him by belittling him as just a shepherd boy.

Despite Eliab's remarks, David remained confident, knowing that the same God who gave him the strength to defeat a lion and a bear would empower him to conquer Goliath. Rather than engaging in an argument with Eliab, David wisely walked away. He didn't waste time trying to prove his worth or defend himself. Instead, he stayed focused on the task God had set before him—the defeat of Goliath.

Had David allowed himself to be distracted by Eliab's words, he might have missed the opportunity to make history and fulfill his destiny. This story reminds us of the importance of walking away from unnecessary conflicts. Engaging in arguments or trying to have the last word often stems from insecurity, and it can pull us off course from what truly matters.

We must choose to focus on our purpose, trusting in who we are and what God is aligning us to achieve. Stay grounded in faith, and let God guide you toward your destiny, undistracted by negativity or doubt. Walk confidently into what He has prepared for you!

Week 27 Friday

Destined For Greatness!

"Then the men of Judah came, and there they anointed David king over the house of Judah." (2 Samuel 2:4, NKJV)

At just seventeen, David was anointed to become the king of Israel—a monumental calling that likely felt distant and unclear. As a shepherd tending sheep, he had no blueprint for kingship, no royal lineage to guide him, and no taste of what it meant to live in such a role. After being anointed, David didn't step into leadership immediately; instead, he returned to his humble duties in the fields. It took thirteen years of preparation before he would ascend to the throne.

David's journey reminds us that when God gives a promise, He will bring it to pass in His perfect timing. During the waiting season, God equips us, aligning us with the right people, offering glimpses of our purpose, and training us through the challenges we encounter. These moments are opportunities to grow, refine our character, and prepare for the role He has destined for us.

David may not have celebrated or fully understood what being anointed meant, but he remained faithful to the path God placed before him. We, too, are called to trust God's process, even when it feels slow or uncertain. Guard the vision He has placed in your heart, stay steadfast in your faith, and hold onto the promise that your time will come.

Let David's story inspire you to trust in God's timing. The preparation may be long, but His plans for you are greater than you can imagine. Stay faithful—your season of fulfillment awaits!

Week 28 Monday

Embrace Freedom!

"Yet now he has reconciled you to himself through the death of Christ in his physical body. As a result, he has brought you into his own presence, and you are holy and blameless as you stand before him without a single fault."
(Colossians 1:22, NLT)

One of the biggest challenges many people face is the weight of regret—past mistakes, wrong choices, hurtful accusations, or even the fear of what others might think of us. These feelings can lead to guilt and self-condemnation, creating an emotional burden that grows heavier over time. As we age, these old wounds often resurface, like shadows that refuse to fade. We may find ourselves blaming others, circumstances, or even ourselves.

But to truly heal, we must embrace forgiveness—both for ourselves and for those who may have wronged us. Letting go of the past is the key to finding peace and freedom from emotional wounds. Remember, God has already forgiven you, wrapped you in His love, and reconciled you to Himself.

It's time to release the burden of your past and step into the freedom God has for you. Picture the weight of guilt and regret falling to the ground, leaving you unencumbered and renewed. By accepting God's forgiveness, you'll find the courage to forgive yourself and others, allowing His peace to fill your heart.

Today, take a step toward letting go of the past. Embrace the inner freedom that comes from knowing you are loved, forgiven, and cherished by God. Move forward with confidence, trusting in His promise to make all things new. You are His beloved, and your future is full of hope.

Week 28 Tuesday

He Enjoys The Smile!

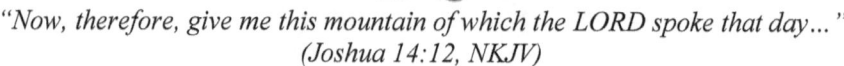

"Now, therefore, give me this mountain of which the LORD spoke that day..."
(Joshua 14:12, NKJV)

The struggles we face may sometimes make us feel as though life is robbing us of our dreams. The wrong choices, setbacks, regrets, mistakes, and missteps can weigh heavily on our hearts. Yet, Caleb's story reminds us that God never forgets the promises He has made or the dreams He's placed within us. At eighty-five years old, Caleb heard God reaffirm the promise that he was not forgotten and would enter the Promised Land. Despite being kept from it for forty years, Caleb remained obedient and courageous, trusting in God's faithfulness.

Like Caleb, we may have moments of doubt, wondering if the dreams we hold dear will ever come to fruition. But God is always working behind the scenes. He watches our attitudes, shapes our character, and waits for the perfect moment when everything will align. When the time is right, God ensures that His plans for us fall beautifully into place.

God delights in your joy. He celebrates your victories, treasures the smile on your face, and desires to dance with you in celebration of what's to come. He will never disappoint you. So, stay faithful, keep your heart fixed on His promises, and push forward with hope. No matter the struggles, trust that your breakthrough is near. The dreams God has placed in your heart will come to life, and His plan for you will exceed anything you could imagine. Keep believing—your time is coming!

Week 28 Wednesday

In The Right Hands!

"O Israel, can I not do to you as this potter has done to his clay? As the clay is in the potter's hand, so are you in my hand." (Jeremiah 18:6, NLT)

Many people feel a sense of disappointment as they transition from one stage of life to another. Thoughts of not having accomplished enough, not earning as much as they hoped, being unsettled in their career, struggling in relationships, or feeling disconnected socially can weigh heavily on the heart. It's easy to focus on what's lacking and feel as though time is slipping away.

But take heart—we serve a God who is always ready to work with us. He is the potter, and we are His clay. With infinite care and wisdom, He shapes and moulds us to fulfill the unique destiny He designed for our lives. If God has placed desires in your heart, trust that He is more than able to bring them to reality. His timing is perfect, and His plans exceed anything we can imagine.

God can open doors overnight, connecting you with the right people, granting you the wisdom, strength, and direction needed to bring your dreams to life. As you trust in Him, your confidence will grow, and you'll find yourself stepping forward with boldness and joy.

Let God do what He does best—trust Him to shape your life with His loving hands. Surrender your worries and let Him guide you to the extraordinary future He has prepared for you. You'll stand amazed at the beautiful results when you place your life in the hands of the Master Potter!

Week 28 Thursday

Everything He Has Is For Us!

"My son,' the father said, 'you are always with me, and everything I have is yours. But we had to celebrate and be glad because this brother of yours was dead and is alive again; he was lost and is found.'" (Luke 15:31–32, NIV)

The story of the prodigal son is a beautiful illustration of God's boundless grace and love. When the wayward son returned home, his father ran to embrace him, overwhelmed with joy. He celebrated his return with a grand feast, but the older brother felt anger and resentment. He couldn't understand why his father honored someone who had made poor choices, while he, who had remained faithful, received no such celebration.

This story mirrors our own struggles at times. We may find ourselves carrying bitterness or envy when others—who seem undeserving—are recognized or blessed. These feelings can weigh us down, robbing us of the joy and peace God desires for us.

But let's not forget the profound words of the father to the older son: *"You are always with me, and everything I have is yours."* This is God's promise to us as His faithful children. He sees our dedication, our sacrifices, and our steadfastness. His blessings and favor are already ours, even if they don't always come with grand celebrations.

God's provision is perfect, and He knows exactly what we need. Rather than comparing ourselves to others, we can rest in the assurance that He sees our faithfulness and delights in blessing us. Let go of resentment, and embrace the joy of knowing that you are deeply loved and richly provided for by your Heavenly Father. Trust in His unwavering goodness, and let your heart be free.

Week 28 Friday

God Will Never Lie!

"...being fully persuaded that God had power to do what he had promised." (Romans 4:21, NIV)

A powerful scripture reminds us of Abraham, who was fully persuaded that God would fulfill His promises. Against all odds, Abraham and Sarah were blessed with their son Isaac when Abraham was one hundred years old—proof that nothing is impossible for God. Their unwavering faith inspires us to trust in God's ability to do the unimaginable, whether it's opening doors, bringing healing, restoring relationships, or pouring favor and blessings into our lives.

Being fully persuaded means holding firm to what we believe, regardless of our circumstances or feelings. It means trusting that God's promises are steadfast and true, never allowing doubt or external influences to shake our faith. When we are fully convinced, we stand resilient, knowing that God's love and faithfulness will never fail.

God is the same yesterday, today, and forever—unchanging, truthful, and all-powerful. He holds every detail of our lives in His hands, and His plans for us are good. No obstacle is too great, no problem beyond His reach, and what He has promised, He is faithful to accomplish.

Let this truth anchor your heart today. Stand firm in the knowledge that nothing can separate you from God's love. Trust Him to work in your life, and watch Him exceed every expectation. With God, all things are possible, and His promises will come to pass. Rest in His faithfulness and let your confidence in Him grow ever stronger. His blessings await!

Week 29 Monday

God Believes In You!

"The angel of the LORD appeared to him and said to him, "The LORD is with you, valiant warrior." (Judges 6:12, NASB)

Gideon was overwhelmed by fear, so much so that he hid in a winepress to avoid his enemies. In that moment of doubt, God sent an angel to remind Gideon of who he truly was. The angel called him a "valiant warrior," even though Gideon felt anything but strong, confident, or prepared for the task ahead. Gideon was called to deliver the people of Israel from the Midianites, but he doubted his abilities and worth. Yet, God saw something greater in him—potential, courage, and a divine purpose.

The angel's words, *"The LORD is with you, valiant warrior,"* carried a powerful message: God had confidence in Gideon, and Gideon needed to have confidence in himself. This same truth applies to us. When God calls us to a purpose, He doesn't focus on our weaknesses—He focuses on our potential and the great things we are capable of through Him.

We must believe in ourselves and trust in what God sees in us. Our perceived shortcomings should not hold us back, because God equips us for every task He sets before us. He sees purpose, value, and success in you, even when you can't see it yourself. Trust that He will guide and prepare you, doing whatever it takes to lead you to fulfill your calling.

Today, embrace the truth that God believes in you. Step forward in faith, knowing that His strength will carry you, and you are capable of accomplishing all He has assigned you to do.

Week 29 Tuesday

God Will Surprise

"When they got there, they found breakfast waiting for them—fish cooking over a charcoal fire, and some bread." (John 21:9, NLT)

Peter and his men spent an entire night fishing, only to come up empty-handed. As the morning light broke, they made their way back to shore, tired and disappointed. Then, a voice called out to them, "Throw your nets on the right side of the boat." Though they didn't recognize it was Jesus at first, they obeyed—and their nets became so full of fish they could hardly pull them in. When they realized it was Jesus, they hurried to shore to find Him waiting, grilling fish and offering them breakfast. Not only did they receive a miraculous catch, but they were also met with the kindness of fellowship and provision.

This story reminds us of the beauty of persistence and faith. Even when it feels like nothing is happening, God sees your efforts and honours your faithfulness. Just as Peter and his men experienced, all it takes is one open door, one right opportunity, and God's perfect timing for everything to change.

When Jesus is at the center of your circumstances, He doesn't just meet your needs—He exceeds them. He brings blessings and rewards that reflect His love and care for you. Stay steadfast and hopeful, knowing that God delights in surprising us with His goodness in unexpected ways.

Keep trusting, keep pressing forward, and remain faithful. You may feel like your nets are empty now, but God is preparing a catch and a feast beyond what you can imagine. Expect the unexpected—God will surprise you!

Week 29 Wednesday

Ask Big!

"The sun stopped in the middle of the sky and delayed going down about a full day." (Joshua 10:13, NIV)

Joshua's story in battle against five kings and their armies is a powerful testament to faith and boldness. As the sun began to set, Joshua realized he needed more daylight to secure victory and prevent the enemy from rising again to cause future problems. With unwavering conviction, he called out, *"Sun, stand still over Gibeon, and you, moon, over the Valley of Aijalon."* In a miraculous act, God answered Joshua's bold request—the sun stood still, and the moon stopped, delaying the night for nearly an entire day.

This story reminds us that we serve a big God who is able to do the impossible. Just as Joshua stepped out in faith and asked for what seemed unimaginable, we, too, can approach God with bold prayers. He is always willing to hear our requests and intervene with favor and blessings when there is purpose, a sincere will, and trust in His power.

If God was able to make the sun stand still for Joshua, imagine what He can do for you. The doors He can open, the healing He can bring, and the breakthroughs He can create are limitless. Don't hesitate to ask boldly and believe wholeheartedly.

Today, be inspired to trust in God's willingness and greatness. Whatever you're facing, bring it before Him with confidence, knowing that He can do far more than we can ask or imagine. Step into faith, and let God surprise you with His mighty works! Ask big—He is ready to answer.

Week 29 Thursday

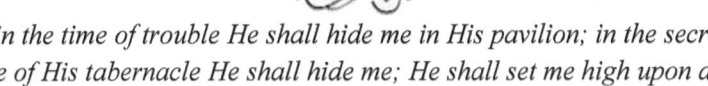

God Provides Self-Care

"For in the time of trouble He shall hide me in His pavilion; in the secret place of His tabernacle He shall hide me; He shall set me high upon a rock." (Psalm 27:5, NKJV)

Life's challenges often leave us yearning for a moment to pause, to breathe, and to practice self-care. Negative thoughts, hurtful words, past traumas, the loss of a loved one, and unexpected difficulties can leave us feeling drained and weary. In those moments, we can find comfort in knowing that God lovingly cares for us, offering us His peace and protection.

Scripture reminds us, *"For in the time of trouble He shall hide me in His pavilion."* Picture a pavilion—a serene, beautiful shelter in a park or garden, offering rest and renewal. This is God's promise to us: a place of refuge where we can find restoration for our souls. Not only that, but He also draws us into the secret place of His Tabernacle, a sacred haven where He keeps us safe and lifts us high upon a rock. From that vantage point, He helps us see that we are above our struggles, secure in His care. Nothing and no one can harm us because we are firmly anchored in His love.

Take heart in this truth today—you are not alone, and you are not defeated. You are on the winning side because your God is always protecting and uplifting you. Let Him be your source of strength, and allow His presence to rejuvenate your spirit. Rest in His pavilion, and embrace the peace that only He can provide. God's love and protection are always with you!

Week 29 Friday

Speak Blessings and Favours

"Death and life are in the power of the tongue, and those who love it and indulge it will eat its fruit and bear the consequences of their words."
(Proverbs 18:21, AMP)

Life can often feel overwhelming when we focus solely on the challenges we face each day. Our daily struggles and distractions can keep us from dreaming and thinking about what our future could look like—a year, three years, or even ten years from now. Yet, what we speak over our lives has the power to shape our direction. Scripture reminds us, *"Death and life are in the power of the tongue,"* encouraging us to speak blessings and favor into our circumstances.

Every word we say holds meaning and influence. When we speak life over areas of hurt, distractions, or challenges—whether it's in relationships, finances, careers, or family dynamics—we invite God's power to transform those situations. By speaking words of hope, healing, and possibility, we align ourselves with God's ability to do the impossible and bring forth blessings beyond our imagination.

It's important to be mindful of what we speak, refusing to let temporary struggles or setbacks dictate our words. Instead, use your voice to declare life, restoration, and abundance. Speak confidently about the desires of your heart and trust in God's ability to fulfill them.

Today, choose to set your heart and words on life. Let your faith inspire your speech, believing that God's plans for you are filled with hope and purpose. Speak boldly and watch as your words, rooted in faith, pave the way for blessings, favor, and a brighter future. Speak life and see the transformation unfold!

Week 30 Monday

God Will Provide!

"For this is what the LORD, the God of Israel, says: There will always be flour and olive oil left in your containers until the time when the LORD sends rain and the crops grow again!" (1 Kings 17:14, NLT)

This is the inspiring story of a widow living during a severe drought, facing unimaginable hardship. With no savings, income, or food, she was down to her last meal. She and her only son prepared themselves to face the end, as they had nothing left to survive. Yet, in the midst of her despair, God sent the prophet Elijah to her. Elijah asked for bread, and despite her dire circumstances, the widow activated her faith instead of dwelling on her poverty. Her unwavering faith unlocked the power of God, who provided for her in a miraculous way.

This story reminds us that God's perspective is vastly different from ours. While we might see only lack, God sees abundance. Where we see emptiness, He sees purpose and value. His promise to His children is clear—He will never forsake the righteous, and provision will come, even if it feels like the eleventh hour.

God blessed the widow so abundantly that she never experienced lack again. This same God who cared for her is still working miracles today. He is faithful to bring hope, sustenance, and blessings into your life when you trust in Him.

Never give up on yourself or on God's ability to intervene. Activate your faith, believing in His power to transform your situation. The blessings He brought to the widow can be yours as well. Trust in His timing, for His provision is always perfect. He will do it again! Keep holding on to faith.

Destined To Be A Hero!

Week 30 Tuesday

"The LORD was with Joseph, so he succeeded in everything he did as he served in the home of his Egyptian master." (Genesis 39:2, NLT)

Like many heroes, it's easy to assume they were simply born extraordinary—gifted, talented, confident, and full of charm. Yet, behind every hero lies a story of struggle, growth, and resilience. Joseph's journey is a perfect example. His story began in betrayal, with his brothers throwing him into a pit and selling him into slavery. From there, he endured false accusations, imprisonment, and isolation. But through it all, Joseph never gave up.

In those difficult and trying times, Joseph didn't allow his circumstances to defeat him. Instead, he used them as opportunities to grow. He took advantage of his disadvantage, sharpening his character, developing wisdom, and gaining the skills and knowledge he needed to fulfill the incredible purpose God had for his life. God's plan for Joseph was far greater than he could have imagined—transforming him from a slave to a trusted leader and hero recognized by Pharaoh himself.

Joseph's faithfulness and perseverance didn't go unnoticed. God honored his unwavering trust and lifted him to a position no ordinary person could fill. His story is a reminder that even in the face of adversity, God is at work, preparing us for something greater.

Stay faithful, no matter the challenges you face. Like Joseph, your perseverance and trust in God can lead to a breakthrough beyond your wildest dreams. Trust that He is working behind the scenes, preparing you for the extraordinary. When the time is right, He will surprise you in ways you never expected.

Week 30 Wednesday

God's Plan Is Unstoppable!

"What then? If some did not believe, their unbelief will not nullify the faithfulness of God, will it?" (Romans 3:3, NASB)

Many times, people may not agree with you or understand the vision God has placed in your heart. Their perspective can be narrow, seeing only from their own vantage point, and this can feel challenging. We long for the support and encouragement of family, friends, and mentors—those closest to us. Yet, not everyone will recognize or embrace the purpose God has given you, and their lack of support can feel discouraging.

Some individuals may even expect you to become dependent on them or seek to take from you rather than pour into your life. But it's important to remember that your destiny is not determined by others' approval. At the end of your earthly journey, it is God to whom you will give an account for what He placed in your heart. His plan for you is personal and unique, and no one knows you better than your Creator.

Even Jesus faced isolation on the cross, without the support of those He had invested in, healed, and performed miracles for. Yet, He remained faithful to His mission. Similarly, you are called to press forward, praying for those who may not stand with you but refusing to let their unbelief deter you from your path.

Don't allow doubt or negativity to distract you from your purpose. Trust in God's unwavering plan for your life. Stay focused, knowing that His promises are secure, and nothing can nullify the destiny He has written for you. God's plan is unstoppable!

Week 30 Thursday

Marked By God!

"At that time Moses was born, and he was no ordinary child."
(Acts 7:20, NIV)

Moses was born with a mark from God—destined for something extraordinary. From a young age, he felt the weight of his calling in his heart. He knew the slavery of the Israelites was wrong and desired to bring change. Though his intentions were good, a misstep led him into hiding for forty years. Yet, even in detours, God's plans never falter. Like Moses, some of us feel the stirrings of a divine calling but may have been distracted or delayed along the way.

I see this same mark of destiny in our children, each uniquely gifted by God. I remember my eldest daughter, my favorite singer, lifting her voice with me in churches. My second daughter, at just two and a half, beamed with joy as she said, "I just saw Jesus. He kissed me and said He is coming back." My third daughter found delight in praying and writing down our prayers. My fourth daughter glowed with excitement, singing her heart out in church. My son, filled with God's presence, knelt beside me in prayer. My fifth daughter shared Jesus with a friend, and my sixth danced for the Lord, radiating joy.

Each of us carries a glimpse of something bigger, a destiny planted by God that will never be canceled. Embrace the excitement of a family walking in the love of the Lord. Speak out the dreams in your heart, and trust God to align your life to fulfill your destiny. When you were born, heaven rejoiced!

Week 30 Friday

Cannot Choose For Others

"Do not be overcome by evil, but overcome evil with good."
(Romans 12:21, NIV)

In today's world, many people choose to live ungodly lives, often finding excuses to avoid church, prayer, and the presence of God. It's easy for them to drift away until life brings unfavorable circumstances. This distance can sometimes lead to unhealthy choices, not just spiritually, but emotionally and physically. When challenges arise, loved ones often step in to provide care, highlighting how our choices impact not just us, but others as well.

Living a godly life and living an ungodly life each carry their own consequences. Scripture reminds us in *"Do not be overcome by evil, but overcome evil with good."* While some may lose sight of this truth and stray far from God's presence, the beauty of His grace is that we are never beyond His reach.

However, we can't make decisions for others—we can only decide for ourselves. It is our choice to follow God, embrace His love, and honor the destiny He has set before us. Staying close to Him allows us to overcome distractions and be anchored in faith.

Today, take responsibility for your choices and focus on living in alignment with God's will. Reflect on His goodness and let it inspire you to stay faithful. Pray for those who are far from His presence, and trust that He can draw them near. You hold the power to decide your path, and through God's strength, you can walk boldly into His promises. The choice is yours—choose Him!

Week 31 Monday

Embrace What God Has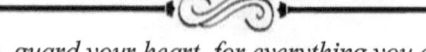

"Above all else, guard your heart, for everything you do flows from it."
(Proverbs 4:23, NIV)

Life's challenges can often stir up negativity, leaving us feeling bitter, angry, upset, or frustrated. These emotions, if left unchecked, can lead to a toxic mindset—a place where trust erodes, resentment takes root, and fear overshadows hope. Scripture reminds us of a crucial truth: *"Above all else, guard your heart, for everything you do flows from it."* Just as bacteria or infection can impact our physical health, wounds to our heart can affect our emotional and spiritual well-being.

Guarding our hearts is essential to keeping negativity at bay. It means protecting ourselves from the hurts and disappointments we experience, refusing to let them linger and fester. When someone wrongs us, our mind may try to convince us that everyone is the same, pushing us toward distrust. But guarding our hearts is about choosing not to allow others' mistakes to define or defeat us.

Start your day with a conscious decision to push away the hurts of the past and release bitterness. Take a step toward embracing what God has for you—His love, His peace, and His blessings. By guarding your heart, you can open yourself to healing and renewal, ready to live in the fullness of His presence.

Let today be a fresh start. Trust in God's power to mend your wounds, lift your spirit, and guide you toward hope and joy. Embrace the life He has for you, knowing that you are deeply loved and cared for. Guard your heart and move forward in faith.

Week 31 Tuesday

God's Blessing Is Long-Term

"After this, Job lived a hundred and forty years; he saw his children and their children to the fourth generation." (Job 42:16, NIV)

Job's story is a remarkable testimony of perseverance and faith in the face of unimaginable adversity. Attacked by the enemy, Job lost everything—his children, his business, his health—and endured accusations from his friends, as well as his wife's discouraging words to curse God and die. The weight of his challenges seemed unbearable, yet Job never gave up on God. Through his steadfast faith, Job held on, trusting in God's plan even in the darkest moments.

After enduring forty-two chapters of trials, God restored Job's life in ways that exceeded his former blessings. He lived another 140 good years, with more children, grandchildren, and even the joy of witnessing four generations after him. God's restoration wasn't just immediate—it had a ripple effect, creating blessings that impacted generations to come.

Job's story encourages us to look beyond our difficulties and see them as distractions from the greater purpose God has for us. Our trials may test us, but they also shape and mature us, strengthening our faith and confidence in the process. God's plans for us always lead to victory, success, and eternal rewards.

Let Job's example inspire you to stay steadfast in your faith, trusting that God will use every challenge to refine you and bring forth blessings. Keep your eyes fixed on Him, and remember that His timing is perfect. Your destiny is in His hands, filled with triumph and abundant joy. Trust in God, and never give up!

Week 31 Wednesday

Fed and Anointed!

"You prepare a table before me in the presence of my enemies; You anoint my head with oil; my cup runs over." (Psalm 23:5, NKJV)

What a beautiful reminder of God's unwavering love for us. Life often brings unexpected challenges—oppositions, hardships, and troubles that threaten to steal our peace. Yet, in the midst of it all, God prepares a table for us. This table is not merely for sustenance but a place to pause, rest, and set aside the worries of the world. It's an invitation to lean on Him, trust Him, and allow His peace to fill our hearts.

When God anoints our heads, it's a powerful declaration of our identity in Him and the strength that resides within us. He reminds us of our position as His beloved children, equipped with His grace and power. We don't need to get angry, fight back, or exhaust ourselves trying to prove our worth. Instead, we can rest in the assurance that God Himself will fight our battles.

Learning to rest in God means trusting Him to bring the best outcomes, knowing He will guide us once we quiet our hearts and allow Him to work. The table He has prepared is not just about provision—it's about anointing us with His peace, calming our spirits, and keeping us secure in His love.

When we embrace this peace, stress gives way to calm, sleepless nights turn into restful ones, and our hearts are filled with serenity. Trust in what God has prepared for you, knowing that His love will carry you through every storm. Rest in Him, and let His peace transform your days.

Week 31 Thursday

Don't Cancel The Blessings!

"He had so many flocks and herds and servants that the Philistines envied him." (Genesis 26:14, NIV)

Isaac's story during the time of famine is a powerful reminder of God's unwavering faithfulness. Despite the difficult circumstances, Isaac planted his crops with determination and trust in the Lord. His faith bore incredible fruit as he reaped a hundredfold harvest—a blessing so abundant that it made him wealthy and even caused the Philistines to envy him. This miraculous provision was a testament to God's hand over his life.

The same God who blessed Isaac is at work today, just as He was then. His desire is to bless us abundantly, not only to meet our needs but also to make us shine as a reflection of His goodness. God's blessings create shifts in both the physical and spiritual realms, setting us apart and allowing His favor to blossom in our lives. He longs for us to prosper, thrive, and stand out as a testimony to His love and provision.

Even when the blessings seem delayed, we must remain patient and faithful. Just as crops and herds take time to grow, God's promises are worth the wait. Continue sowing seeds of faith, trusting that He will bring the harvest at the perfect time. Don't lose hope, even in seasons of famine—your reward is coming.

Let Isaac's story encourage you to stay steadfast in your trust. God's blessings are never canceled, and His timing is always perfect. Keep believing, keep sowing, and watch as the Lord brings forth abundance in your life. Your season of harvest will arrive!

Week 31 Friday

God Will Satisfy Your Thirst!

"For he satisfies the thirsty soul and fills the hungry soul with good."
(Psalm 107:9, TLB)

Kathleen and I embarked on a Dubai desert safari, where the sweltering heat reached 47 degrees Celsius. Under the blazing sun, our natural thirst for water was undeniable—we felt drained and tired. Yet, with every sip we took, satisfaction and renewal followed. This experience brought to light a deeper truth: just as our bodies crave water in the heat, our souls crave the living water of the Lord during the "heat" of life's challenges.

Life often brings moments of uncertainty, setbacks, and struggles that can leave us feeling spiritually dry. There are times when the pressures of life overwhelm us, and panic clouds our thoughts. The obstacles we face may seem to overshadow our dreams, tempting us to believe they'll never come to fruition. But amid this spiritual thirst, God promises to satisfy our souls and fill us with His goodness.

The natural feeling of emptiness is God's opportunity to pour His living water into our hearts, renewing us to the point of overflow. His presence and provision are designed to quench our deepest spiritual thirst and bring us peace and hope.

Whenever life feels overwhelming, remind yourself of God's promise. He is always ready to satisfy your soul, to renew your spirit, and to guide you through the challenges. Like the refreshment of cool water on a hot day, His living water will restore you fully. Embrace this truth and let Him fill you with His endless grace and love!

Week 32 Monday

God Will Answer You!

"I also tell you this: If two of you agree here on earth concerning anything you ask, my Father in heaven will do it for you."
(Matthew 18:19, NLT)

Each of us is uniquely created with dreams, goals, and visions—seeds planted in our hearts by God from the very moment of our creation. As we grow, our personality and character evolve, shaping us to align with those godly desires. However, life often presents challenges, as the enemy seeks to discourage and hold us back from fulfilling our purpose. The good news is that Jesus calls us to the power of prayer, reminding us that through faith, nothing is impossible.

One of the most beautiful truths Jesus taught is the strength that comes when we join our faith with another. As He said, *"If two shall agree..."* there is incredible power in unity and agreement. When facing trials or feeling weary and uncertain, don't carry the weight alone. Find someone to stand with you in prayer, even if your faith feels small. God honors even the tiniest measure of faith and will pour out blessings and favor upon those who seek Him with obedient hearts.

Today, take comfort in knowing that God is ready to meet you in your need. Whatever your prayer may be—healing, financial provision, restored relationships, or new opportunities—trust that He hears you. I join my faith with yours, believing for your breakthrough in Jesus's name. Together, let's stand firm in faith, knowing that our God is faithful to bring His promises to pass. Your blessing is on its way—He is working in your life!

Week 32 Tuesday

God Will Reward You!

"The LORD rewarded me for doing right. He has seen my innocence."
(Psalm 18:24, NLT)

David's reflections on God's faithfulness remind us of His unwavering protection and provision. Throughout his life, David faced powerful enemies, yet God continually rescued him and shielded him from dangers seen and unseen. One constant theme in David's journey was his commitment to doing what was right, even in the face of adversity. This same principle applies to us—we always have the choice to honor God by doing what is right, even when it feels like others are taking advantage of us.

God sees every good deed, every act of kindness, and every faithful decision we make, and He rewards us for it. His favor has a way of turning situations around in surprising and unexpected ways. You may witness His blessings in your children's growth and success, a promotion at work, unexpected discounts while shopping, bills paid by someone's generosity, issues resolved effortlessly, or doors opening where you thought none existed. These moments are glimpses of God's abundant grace poured out in return for your faithfulness.

Stay focused on honoring God and living according to His principles, trusting that He sees and cherishes your efforts. His rewards go beyond our expectations, bringing blessings that enrich every part of our lives. As you continue to do what is right before the Lord, let His favor lead you into a future filled with peace, joy, and unexpected blessings. Trust in His timing, for His rewards are always worth the wait!

Week 32 Wednesday

God Believes In You!

"Not by might nor by power, but by My Spirit," says the LORD Almighty."
(Philippians 4:12–13, NLT)

When Jesus walked this earth, He left a lasting impression everywhere He went. His life was a living reflection of God's nature—full of compassion, grace, and power. Through signs, wonders, and miracles, He demonstrated God's love. He treated everyone with dignity and respect, never overlooking anyone. Even in the midst of busyness, He paused for the woman who touched His garment, acknowledging her faith. Jesus never let His schedule overshadow His mission to touch lives—young and old, rich and poor, broken and whole.

Jesus also prioritized prayer. He spent time with the Father, regaining strength, hearing His guidance, and remaining connected to His purpose. His prayer life was the foundation of the extraordinary impact He had on the world.

What is the Spirit of God saying to you today? Are you prepared to step into the destiny He has designed just for you? The same Spirit that led Jesus dwells in us, equipping us to walk as He walked. If you long to see the supernatural manifest in the natural, Jesus is the perfect example to follow.

Treat people with kindness and love as if today were your last opportunity to make a difference. Honour others, show God's love in your actions, and let His presence shine through your life. Live fully, cherishing every moment and opportunity. When you embrace this calling, you'll reflect the heart of Christ and leave a legacy of love and faith. The Spirit within you is ready to lead you forward!

Week 32 Thursday

Prosper In All Things!

"Beloved, I pray that you may prosper in all things and be in health, just as your soul prospers." (3 John 2, NKJV)

It's easy to lose sight of the need to prosper or take care of our health when life feels overwhelming—when struggles weigh us down or repeated attempts seem to end in failure. Yet, the key to true well-being lies in caring for our soul: the mind, will, and emotions. This deeper care is essential to living a life of fulfillment.

In my book *Soul Care,* I emphasize the importance of healing wounded emotions. Many of us dedicate time, energy, and effort to caring for our physical bodies, striving to look and feel good. However, we often neglect the equally vital task of tending to our soul. Our thoughts, emotions, behaviors, and attitudes profoundly influence how we live and connect with others. A wounded soul struggles to find lasting happiness—it remains guarded, unable to embrace joy or fully enjoy meaningful relationships.

Healing and nurturing the soul is transformative. When we prioritize soul care, we align ourselves with emotional health and spiritual abundance, unlocking the ability to thrive in every area of life. A prosperous soul leads to prosperous living.

Take time to reflect on the state of your soul and seek healing where it's needed. Allow God's presence to restore your inner being, guiding you toward peace, joy, and balance. Remember, when your soul prospers, so will every aspect of your life. Caring for your soul is not just self-care—it's essential to thriving and living a fulfilled life!

Week 32 Friday

God Will Defend Us!

"Finding a fresh jawbone of a donkey, he grabbed it and struck down a thousand men." (Judges 15:15, NIV)

Samson's story is a powerful reminder of how God can use the smallest, most ordinary things to create extraordinary breakthroughs. Surrounded by an army with no help, protection, or weapons, Samson's only resource was the jawbone of a donkey. While it seemed insignificant, God's presence transformed it into a powerful tool. With that jawbone, Samson struck down 1,000 men, achieving a miraculous victory that only God could bring.

We all face struggles—unexpected challenges and situations beyond our control. It's easy to feel frustrated, disappointed, or defeated when it seems like we lack the support or resources we need. But let Samson's story remind you that no problem is too great for God. He can use whatever is in your hands—no matter how small or ordinary it may seem—to bring about your breakthrough. When His presence is with you, even the simplest things can become instruments of His power.

Don't waste energy comparing yourself to others or feeling sorry for what you don't have. Instead, focus on who lives within you. The presence of God is your greatest strength and resource. Trust Him to take what you have and turn it into something extraordinary. Stay rooted in faith and lean into His power. With God working in and through you, there's no limit to what you can overcome. Keep your eyes on Him, not on what's around you, and watch His miracles unfold in your life!

Week 33 Monday
Enjoy The War!

"Walk by the Spirit, and you will not gratify the desires of the flesh. For the flesh desires what is contrary to the Spirit, and the Spirit what is contrary to the flesh. They are in conflict with each other, so that you are not to do whatever you want." (Galatians 5:16–17, NIV)

We all carry a "thorn in the flesh," those struggles that resurface time and again—cravings, temptations, negative thinking, or wounds from past hurts. These challenges remind us of our humanity, but the real problem arises when we start to believe we're perfect, seeing faults in others while ignoring our own. The flesh can manifest in pride, weaknesses, or even manipulation, drawing us away from the life God desires for us.

Scripture reminds us there's a war within us—a constant battle between the flesh and the spirit. While this struggle can feel disheartening, it's also a sign that we're on the right path. Those who no longer feel this inner conflict may have become blinded by pride, believing they've reached perfection. But the war within reveals our need to grow in the spirit and depend on God.

God invites us to lean on Him, to trust Him to guide our steps and keep the path of life open until our journey on this earth is complete.

Today, make the choice to walk closely with God. Trust Him to take you places you never imagined, opening doors to unexpected blessings and favor. In His presence, you'll find the strength to rise above the struggles of the flesh and live a life filled with His grace and love.

Week 33 Tuesday

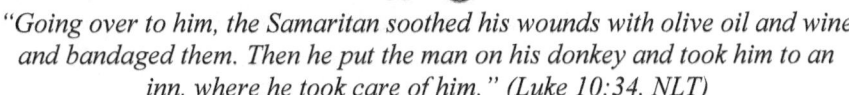

God Has Assignments!

"Going over to him, the Samaritan soothed his wounds with olive oil and wine and bandaged them. Then he put the man on his donkey and took him to an inn, where he took care of him." (Luke 10:34, NLT)

The story of the Good Samaritan, shared by Jesus, is a timeless lesson about compassion and selfless love. On his journey, the Samaritan encountered a man who had been beaten and left for dead on the side of the road. Without hesitation, he placed the man on his donkey and took him to a safe place where he could recover. Not only did the Samaritan provide immediate care, but he also covered the costs for the man's ongoing treatment. This act of kindness wasn't transactional—it was God's assignment for the Samaritan, who responded with a willing and open heart. In turn, God blessed him richly.

Though the story doesn't reveal the aftermath between the Samaritan and the man he helped, the message is clear. God calls us to be like Him, reaching out to those in need—the broken, the hurting, and those searching for hope. Through us, He can bring healing, encouragement, and transformation to others' lives. We are His vessels for change and blessing.

As believers, it's our duty to embrace these divine assignments without expecting anything in return. There's no need for recognition or applause; simply fulfill what God places before you with humility and love. When we walk in obedience and selflessness, God rewards us in ways that are beyond our imagination. Your life will overflow with favor and blessings as you honor His calling. Be the Good Samaritan today, letting God's love shine through you!

Week 33 Wednesday

A Host With Us!

"Since we are surrounded by such a great cloud of witnesses, let us throw off everything that hinders and the sin that so easily entangles. And let us run with perseverance the race marked out for us, fixing our eyes on Jesus, the pioneer and perfecter of faith. For the joy set before Him He endured the cross, scorning its shame, and sat down at the right hand of the throne of God.")Hebrews 12:1–2, NIV

Watching children play soccer is always a joyful and entertaining experience. Seeing them on the field often brings back memories of playing in my own school days. Back then, there were no parents or spectators on the sidelines, but today, our children have the support of cheering families and community members. Their encouragement creates an atmosphere of love and motivation, something we might long for in our own spiritual journeys.

In our walk with God, it's not uncommon to feel alone, as if no one is there to cheer us on. However, scripture reminds us that we are surrounded by a great cloud of witnesses, urging us to press forward. Though life's challenges may cause us to stumble and fall, even a thousand times, the key is to get up each time and run with perseverance the race set before us.

Jesus is our ultimate example of endurance and faith. By fixing our eyes on Him, we are reminded that we are never truly alone. An entire host of heaven is cheering us on, believing in us to finish strong. Embrace the encouragement of this truth and keep moving forward, knowing that eternity holds a beautiful reunion with those who cheer you on!

Week 33 Thursday

A Channel For Blessing!

"From the day Joseph was put in charge of his master's household and property, the LORD began to bless Potiphar's household for Joseph's sake. All his household affairs ran smoothly, and his crops and livestock flourished." (Genesis 39:5, NLT)

We all need to embrace the truth of this scripture. God has uniquely positioned us in various jobs, relationships, social circles, sports, hobbies, and congregations. He has blessed each of us with gifts and talents so we can be an influence and a source of blessings to others. However, insecurities and lack of confidence in those around us may sometimes arise, causing others to feel threatened or resistant. These feelings can disrupt the flow of God's plan, but we must remain steadfast.

If others don't recognize or accept the gifts God has placed in you, don't let it discourage you. Dust off your feet and keep moving forward, trusting that God has an assignment for your life. The scripture reminds us, *"From the day Joseph was put in charge of his master's household and property, the LORD began to bless Potiphar's household for Joseph's sake."* Just as Joseph's faithfulness brought blessings to Potiphar, God will use you as a channel of blessings wherever you are.

Your gifts and presence can bring favor to businesses, families, friendships, and communities. Trust God's timing and wait for the appointed moment to step into your calling. Don't let obstacles or doubts hold you back—God will use you to bless others in extraordinary ways!

Week 33 Friday

God Always Has A Plan!

"Cast your cares on the LORD, and He will sustain you; He will never let the righteous be shaken."(Psalm 55:22, NIV)

We all wrestle with waiting on God's timing, especially in a fast-paced world where everything seems to demand instant results. It's easy to feel frustrated and impatient when things don't happen as quickly as we'd like. But God's timing is perfect, and He is always in control. Often, our emotions and feelings cloud our perspective, making it hard to trust that He is working behind the scenes for our good.

It was like a light bulb moment for me when I realized that God knows what tomorrow holds and is already preparing a plan for every challenge the enemy might bring. When we mess up, He has a plan. When the enemy attacks, He has a plan. When we feel overwhelmed, depressed, or like failures, He has a plan. Even when it seems like no one understands or the situation feels never-ending, God still has a plan.

Instead of chasing after fleeting solutions, we can rest in the truth that God holds our future in His hands. Worry only wastes our energy. Trusting God allows us to step back and watch Him work wonders in His perfect timing. His Word assures us that He will never let the righteous be shaken.

Let this reminder bring peace to your heart today. God's plans are always for your good, and His timing, though different from ours, is unfailingly perfect. Trust Him, and you'll see His blessings unfold in ways beyond what you could imagine.

Week 34 Monday

God Will Not Turn His Back!

"God heard the boy crying..." (Genesis 21:17, NIV)

Ishmael's story is a powerful testament to God's unwavering love and care for us. At just sixteen years old, Ishmael found himself in the desert with his mother, feeling abandoned, rejected, and confused. He was out of food and water, caught in the consequences of choices he could not control—a by product of the complicated relationship between his mother, Abraham, and Sarah. In today's world, his upbringing might be seen as dysfunctional. Despite it all, Ishmael's cries reached the Lord, and God heard him.

This story beautifully reflects who God is—faithful and compassionate, even in the midst of pain, betrayal, and difficult circumstances. Regardless of the mistakes, regrets, or wrong choices of others, God never turns His back on us. He is fully aware of the hurt we carry and is ready to turn situations around for good.

Let Ishmael's experience inspire you to trust that God sees your worth and the greatness within you. Don't let the decisions or actions of others define your identity or hold you back. God's plans for you are far greater than any obstacle. He is always ready to work in your life, bringing healing, restoration, and hope.

You are not defined by the struggles you've faced or the choices others have made. You are defined by the love of a God who sees your potential and desires to bless you abundantly. Hold onto this truth—you have greatness in you!

Week 34 Tuesday

My Redeemer Lives!

"But as for me, I know that my Redeemer lives, and he will stand upon the earth at last." (Job 19:25, NLT)

Job's story is one of perseverance, faith, and a profound transformation. Despite being blameless, he endured unimaginable trials—losing his business, his children, and his health. At first, Job felt discouraged and disappointed, and he may have even struggled with bitterness toward God. But his journey didn't end there. Job chose to turn his thoughts around, recondition his mind, and restructure his thinking. It was this powerful shift in perspective that marked a turning point in his life. The moment Job changed his mindset, God blessed him abundantly, restoring far more than he had lost.

This story teaches us the importance of addressing the root cause of the challenges we face. We must believe wholeheartedly that God is with us and capable of helping us through every trial, no matter how big or small. If we let time pass without seeking His help, bitterness can take root, and we may grow numb to unhealthy patterns, allowing abnormalities to feel normal.

Job's declaration, *"I know that my Redeemer lives,"* is an inspiring reminder of the power of faith and hope. When we choose to shift our thinking and trust in God's presence, we open the door to His blessings and peace. Let Job's story encourage you to embrace hope and trust in the Redeemer who lives and works on your behalf. Through Him, your situation can turn around, bringing restoration and joy beyond your expectations. Hold on—God has a plan for you!

Week 34 Wednesday

God Thinks Highly Of You!

"He has reconciled you to Himself through the death of Christ in His physical body. As a result, He has brought you into His own presence, and you are holy and blameless as you stand before Him without a single fault. But you must continue to believe this truth and stand firmly in it. Don't drift away from the assurance you received when you heard the Good News . . ."
(Colossians 1:22–23, NLT)

Life often presents challenges that can leave us feeling bitter, angry, and hesitant to trust others. At times, we may even struggle to love ourselves, burdened by past mistakes, wrong choices, and the hurts we carry. This inner conflict can create a sense that something is broken within us, causing us to become our own worst enemy. Such feelings not only affect us personally but also ripple into our relationships with loved ones—spouses, children, and friends. Negative thoughts shape how we view ourselves and the world, holding us back from experiencing the fullness of life.

To move forward, we need to shift our focus. Instead of dwelling on what we perceive as wrong with us, let's celebrate what is right. Let's recognize our strengths rather than fixating on our weaknesses. Constantly replaying negativity in our minds will only keep us stuck. It's through God's presence that we find true healing and acceptance.

Scripture reminds us that when we stand before God, we are holy, blameless, and without a single fault. Learning to live in this freedom takes time, but it begins with trusting God's love for us.

Release the burden of self-doubt and step into the fullness of His grace. You are cherished, valued, and deeply loved. Focus on your blessings, and let God's presence guide you toward a life of joy, peace, and confidence.

Week 34 Thursday

You Carry Greatness!

"Walk with the wise and become wise; associate with fools and get in trouble." (Proverbs 13:20, NLT)

In recent years, this scripture has taken on a deeper meaning. When we are young, we often don't think about the cost of who we spend time with. We seek acceptance and go along with the crowd, not realizing how much energy can be drained by being with the wrong people. It's only later, upon reflection, that we see how much time was wasted on relationships that didn't nurture or uplift us.

We may think that by listening to or spending time with negative, toxic individuals, we are helping them. Yet, many of these individuals are trapped in cycles of loneliness and emptiness, spending much of their time sharing problems rather than seeking solutions. While compassion is important, we must also recognize the value of protecting our own peace and energy.

You carry seeds of greatness within you, and they deserve to be nurtured and guarded. Surround yourself with wise, uplifting individuals who lead positive and fruitful lives. Godliness shines brightly and brings the favor and blessings of the Lord. As you choose to spend time with quality people who inspire and encourage you, you'll notice a beautiful shift—a life overflowing with joy, purpose, and fulfillment.

Prioritize relationships that honor the greatness God has placed in you. Your time and energy are precious. Invest them wisely, and watch the blessings of connection, happiness, and growth come alive in your life!

Week 34 Friday

Don't Be Distracted

"And Caleb silenced the people before Moses and said, "Surely, let us go up and let us take possession of it because surely we will be able to prevail over it." (Numbers 13:30, LEB)

When Moses sent twelve men to explore the Promised Land, ten returned with fear in their hearts. They saw giants in the land, towering and strong, and they could only focus on the fortified cities that seemed impossible to conquer. They couldn't envision themselves ever succeeding and believed defeat was inevitable. However, Joshua and Caleb, the other two men, came back with a completely different perspective. They had no doubts that they could overcome the giants and take possession of the land. Their faith and trust in God set them apart, and ultimately, they were the only two from that generation who entered the Promised Land.

This story reminds us not to let fear or obstacles talk us out of our dreams, goals, and visions. Giants may appear intimidating, but we must look beyond them. If God has placed a dream in your heart and given you a vision for your future, He will make a way to bring it to reality—no matter how impossible it may seem. Every challenge is an opportunity for God to demonstrate His power.

Trust Him and move forward with confidence, knowing He is with you. Don't let the sight of giants distract you from the greatness God has planned. Keep your focus on Him, and you will see His promises come to life. Step boldly in faith, and watch as He turns the impossible into the miraculous! Giants are no match for the God who holds your future.

Week 35 Monday
Change Your Name!

"God also said to Abraham, "As for Sarai your wife, you are no longer to call her Sarai; her name will be Sarah." (Genesis 17:15, NIV)

Sarai was ninety years old and still longing for the one thing she thought was impossible—a child. For over seventy years, she might have carried thoughts like, "I am barren; I can't have a child," or "Why me? What is wrong with me?" Watching her friends raise families likely deepened her pain, leaving her feeling unworthy and unloved by God. She may have wrestled with years of self-defeating thoughts and doubts. But God had not forgotten Sarai.

When God promised her and Abram a son, He didn't just give them a promise; He gave them new identities. Sarai became Sarah, and Abram became Abraham. With these new names came new hope and purpose. Sarah's name means princess or noblewoman—a reflection of the greatness God saw in her, even when she couldn't see it in herself. Though she may not have felt worthy to birth a bloodline, God saw her differently, and His promise came to pass.

Like Sarah, we too must step away from doubt, fear, and negativity. We must choose to replace lies with truth and see ourselves as God sees us—full of purpose and potential. Speak life over yourself. Give yourself a name that declares victory, joy, and accomplishment—a name that reflects who God has called you to be. Let His promises redefine your life, just as they did for Sarah. You are destined for greatness, and your name should reflect the incredible journey He has planned for you!

Week 35 Tuesday

Winning A Lottery

"Patient endurance is what you need now so that you will continue to do God's will. Then you will receive all that he has promised."
(Hebrews 10:36, NLT)

As we grow and gain a deeper understanding of how life works, we begin to realize the vital role patience plays. As children, we often had our needs met quickly—our parents did their best to provide what we wanted. However, as we mature and take on responsibilities, we learn that achieving our dreams, goals, and desires takes time and perseverance. Many things in life require patience, especially when the path ahead seems long and uncertain.

It's during these seasons of waiting that patience is most important—a time when we trust God wholeheartedly, even when circumstances or others around us seem discouraging. Our minds may be tempted to waver or adjust our goals, but God calls us to remain steadfast. Trusting Him with patience opens the door to breakthroughs, blessings, and favor beyond what we can imagine. With time, we see His promises come to life, like uncovering a treasure we've long awaited.

Patience is a powerful tool to align us with God's perfect timing. While waiting is never easy, the rewards are more than worth it. Keep trusting Him, no matter how impossible things may seem. If God has placed a promise in your heart, He will bring it to fruition. Don't give up—He is faithful, and His plans for you are filled with hope, joy, and victory. Trust that what He says, He will do, and let patience carry you into the fulfillment of His promises!

Week 35 Wednesday

God Will Bless You!

"When Isaac planted his crops that year, he harvested a hundred times more grain than he planted, for the LORD blessed him." (Genesis 26:12, NLT)

Isaac's story during a time of great famine is a beautiful example of trusting God and stepping out in faith. Living among the Philistines in drought-stricken conditions, Isaac chose to plant seeds despite the odds. His faith and obedience brought remarkable blessings, as God provided him with a hundredfold harvest. Isaac's wealth grew, his herds and flocks flourished, and the blessings poured out over his life were so abundant that they stirred jealousy among the Philistines.

This story reminds us to remain steadfast in pursuing what God has placed in our hearts, regardless of the challenges or uncertainties we face. God calls us to step out boldly, trusting Him to step in and work through our faith in the unknown. While others may misunderstand, become envious, or feel unsettled by your obedience, these concerns should not deter you.

As God blessed Isaac, He desires to bless you in extraordinary ways. Your "seed" may take many forms—a prayer for your marriage, an act of love for your children, support for a mission trip, humanitarian aid, or even encouragement to a friend. Whatever it is, sow it with confidence, knowing that God's power is activated through faith and action.

Let Isaac's example inspire you to move beyond your comfort zone and trust God's provision. When we step out in faith, His blessings overflow, opening doors we never imagined. Trust Him today—your harvest is waiting!

Week 35 Thursday

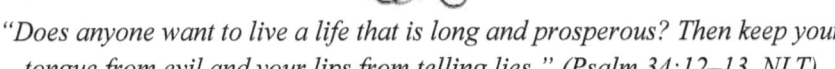
Live Long and Prosperous!

"Does anyone want to live a life that is long and prosperous? Then keep your tongue from evil and your lips from telling lies." (Psalm 34:12–13, NLT)

This scripture provides such a clear and powerful reminder of what it takes to live a long and prosperous life. While many of us focus on physical health—eating right, exercising, and resting—we must also remember the importance of the words we speak. The Bible encourages us to guard our tongues, refraining from speaking evil, sharing negative words, or telling lies.

At times, we may think, "I don't lie," but often, we unintentionally lie to ourselves. Thoughts like "I'm not good enough," "I'll never be great," "Nobody cares about me," or "I have nothing to offer" are subtle yet harmful lies. These self-defeating thoughts are a form of speaking defeat over our own lives, dimming the light of the potential God has placed within us.

Instead, we're called to speak life. We should declare blessings over ourselves and trust in the favor and goodness of God to surround us. By aligning our perspective with God's, we can see ourselves the way He sees us—worthy, capable, and loved. This shift in mindset sets us on the path to the prosperous and fulfilling life He desires for us.

Let's make the choice today to speak positivity and truth over ourselves. Embrace the promises of God and the greatness He has placed within you. Words have power—use them to build a life filled with hope, joy, and abundance. You are destined for greatness, and speaking life is your key to living it!

Week 35 Friday

Tread Down Our Enemies!

"Through God we will do valiantly, for it is He who shall tread down our enemies." (Psalm 60:12, NKJV)

From the very moment of conception, we are caught in a battle. The enemy seeks to steal, kill, and destroy because he knows God has a great destiny for every soul. Yet we are never alone in this fight—God is our defender, our shield, and our source of strength. Just as an army surrounds and protects, there are far more with us than against us. God stands for us and promises to tread down our enemies.

If you're feeling under attack—whether it's in your finances, relationships, or mind—remember, it's only an attack, not the end of your story. God will not let the enemy destroy you, especially when His destiny for your life is yet to unfold. His plans for you are greater than any challenge you face.

It's crucial to align your life with God. Call upon Him, seek His guidance, and ask for His protection. Remaining in His presence keeps us under His wings of refuge and safety. Don't let the demands of life pull you away from your relationship with Him. Stay close to Him, trust in His promises, and rely on His strength.

Your victory is certain because God is fighting for you. He will turn the attack into a testimony of His power and faithfulness. Stay anchored in Him, and watch as He brings you through, stronger than ever. God will tread down your enemies and lead you to triumph!

Week 36 Monday

God Will Payback!

, "If the God of my father had not been on my side—the God of Abraham and the fearsome God of Isaac—you would have sent me away empty-handed. But God has seen your abuse and my hard work." (Genesis 31:42, NLT)

Jacob's story is a powerful reminder of the blessings that come from perseverance and faithfulness. Despite being cheated and lied to by his father-in-law Laban, who altered his wages ten times, Jacob continued to work diligently and wholeheartedly. He chose not to focus on the injustice but instead kept his trust in the God of Abraham and Isaac, knowing that God was on his side. Jacob's unwavering faith led to immense blessings—God rewarded him with a greater flock and abundance far beyond Laban's. His faithfulness opened the door to restoration and overflow.

This example encourages us to keep going, even when it feels like we're not getting what we deserve or facing unfair treatment. God sees every effort, every moment of hard work, and every injustice we endure. He is faithful to bring payback and blessings at the right time. The Bible assures us, *"But God has seen your abuse and my hard work."* This truth reminds us that God will not overlook our struggles; He will bring sudden blessings, unexpected favor, open doors, and promotions. What feels lost will be restored.

Stay focused on God's ability, not on the actions of others. His plans for you are bigger than any obstacle or unfairness. Trust Him to bring forth blessings that surpass your expectations. Keep your faith strong, and let God turn every challenge into a testimony of His goodness. You'll regain more than you ever thought possible!

Week 36 Tuesday

Keep The Window Open!

"For we must always cherish the words of our Lord Jesus, who taught, 'Giving brings a far greater blessing than receiving.'" (Acts 20:35, TPT)

Many people find it much easier to receive than to give. The mindset of "what can I get" often feels natural, while the question of "what can I give" may not come as readily. Over time, we may even develop an expectation that others will give, pay the bill, or handle a situation. Yet the true calling is to shift our perspective—asking instead, "How can I help?" or "What can I do to assist?"

If we want to experience the favor and overflowing blessings of God, we must cultivate a heart that loves to give. Scripture reminds us that giving brings more blessings than receiving. Generosity opens the door for financial growth, deeper relationships, and personal fulfillment. As we learn to give selflessly, we begin to see who God created us to be—and with it, an appreciation for the value of our lives.

Every act of giving keeps the window of heaven open over us, allowing God's blessings to flow into our lives. Giving doesn't just impact others; it transforms us, bringing joy and purpose to our hearts.

Let this reminder encourage you to embrace a lifestyle of generosity. Whether it's lending a hand, offering support, or sharing resources, your giving has the power to create change. With each act of love and kindness, you'll witness God's blessings unfold in unimaginable ways. Give from the heart and see the beauty of God's favor alive in your life!

Week 36 Wednesday

God Will Reimburse Us!

"Whatever you do, work at it with all your heart, as working for the Lord, not for human masters, since you know you will receive an inheritance from the Lord as a reward. It is the Lord Christ you are serving."
(Colossians 3:23–24, NIV)

In today's fast-paced world, it often feels like everything and everyone demands something from us. Over time, a culture has emerged where many aim to do the bare minimum just to get by. Pride in our work, relationships, and personal growth has faded for some, and cutting corners has become all too common—whether at our jobs, with friends and family, or even in our own lives. Yet, scripture reminds us that in everything we do, we should work at it wholeheartedly, as if working for the Lord.

This call applies to every aspect of life—our relationships, education, careers, spiritual growth, and every path we take. We don't work for the approval of bosses or authority figures; rather, we work as unto God, trusting that He sees and rewards our efforts. Past hurts and wrongs should not deter us, for God promises to care for those who have treated us unfairly and to restore what has been lost.

Let this truth encourage you: every act of faithfulness is seen by the Lord. He promises an inheritance and blessings for those who serve Him with a heart of devotion. Keep pushing forward, knowing that you serve Christ, who will bless your efforts and reward you abundantly. Don't let past setbacks or wrongs hold you back—trust that God will take care of every detail. When you work for Him, your life becomes a testimony of His grace and favor!

Week 36 Thursday

God Will Set You Up!

"When Mary reached the place where Jesus was and saw him, she fell at his feet and said, "Lord, if you had been here, my brother would not have died." (John 11:32, NIV)

Jesus shared a close bond with Lazarus, Mary, and Martha, yet even His dear friend fell ill and passed away. By the time Jesus arrived, Lazarus had been buried for three days. This story resonates deeply with our own experiences—those moments when it feels like Jesus isn't showing up, when hope fades and expectations crumble. Like Mary, we may feel disappointed, wondering why our struggles seem unanswered.

Life presents many challenges that can feel like they've reached a dead end, much like Lazarus's situation. Yet, God's timing is never random; it is deliberate and filled with purpose. He may allow delays or outcomes that seem unfavorable because His plans are far greater than we can imagine. When Lazarus died, God was orchestrating something miraculous—to raise him from the dead after three days and reveal His divine power.

This story encourages us to let go of our fears and trust God completely. He is never late, and He is always working for our good. What may seem like an impossible situation is often a setup for a breakthrough that glorifies His name and blesses us abundantly.

Stay faithful in the face of challenges, remembering that God's plans are perfect. He will transform your struggles into powerful testimonies of His love and strength. Trust Him to use your circumstances as a means to declare His power and bring blessings into your life! God's timing is always worth the wait.

Week 36 Friday

Yourself and Your Family

"The LORD bless you and keep you; the LORD make his face shine on you and be gracious to you; the LORD turn his face toward you and give you peace." (Numbers 6:24–26, NIV)

This example provides such a powerful reminder for us to follow. It is so easy to fall into the habit of speaking negatively about ourselves and others. However, negative words have the power to block or delay God's best for our lives, altering our path and allowing toxicity to take root in our minds. Instead, we must intentionally bless ourselves and others by declaring what God's Word says.

A beautiful practice is to start each day by speaking blessings over your life. Declare, *"I bless myself with the goodness of God to pursue and overtake me, with favor in high places, with wisdom, direction, and renewed strength. I align my destiny with God's plan to prosper. I will connect with the right people at the right time. Lord, let Your face shine upon me, granting me great vision to fulfill the destiny You have designed for me."*

Extend these blessings to your family as well, speaking life, protection, and success over them: *"I declare favor upon my children and spouse. I speak protection, provision, and promotion over their lives. May they prosper, be in good health, and see fruitfulness in all they do."*

Your words hold incredible power—use them to cancel out negativity and speak hope, joy, and abundance into existence. Bless yourself and your loved ones daily, trusting that God's favor will overflow in every area of your life. Words of blessing unlock doors of possibility!

Week 37 Monday

God Will Do It!

"Be on your guard; stand firm in the faith; be courageous; be strong." (1 Corinthians 16:13, NIV)

In October 1996, God spoke a powerful word to me—that my sons-in-law would be like sons to me. Over the years, I held tightly to that promise, guarding it in my heart and relying on God's wisdom to direct the necessary structures and plans. Today, I am blessed to see His word fulfilled—my sons-in-law are truly like sons. This journey has taught me so much about standing firm in faith.

God doesn't require extraordinary faith; He asks us to stand unwavering in our belief in what He has spoken. Doubts and fears may try to creep in, but we must guard against them. Even when it feels like everything is falling apart or what we're believing for seems distant, we are called to hold steadfast. Stand like a bystander, keeping your eyes fixed on the One who made the promise.

When God spoke to me, His word pierced my heart like a bullet. I carried that promise with unwavering trust, knowing He would fulfill it in His perfect timing. Each son-in-law was uniquely brought to our daughters, handpicked by God to ensure His word came to life.

This story reminds us to trust God's ability and faithfulness. When He speaks, He is more than capable of delivering. Let us stand firm in faith, guarding against doubts and holding onto His promises. God's words are true, and His plans never fail. Keep your faith strong and witness His blessings unfold!

Week 37 Tuesday

Learn To Fight!

"Fight the good fight of the faith." (1 Timothy 6:12, NIV)

If you are going to fight, make sure you fight to win. The fight we are called to isn't physical; it's spiritual. People often fight when their boundaries are crossed, when they disagree, or when they feel the need to defend themselves. But God encourages us to approach challenges differently. Instead of letting difficulties or adverse circumstances lead us to complaining or frustration, we are called to fight through prayer and supplication. This is the good fight of faith.

When we fight this way, we prepare ourselves for God's favor, greater anointing, increased strength, and the confidence to step into the opportunities He has prepared for us. Through the challenges we face, God shapes us to become stronger, wiser, and more equipped to fulfill His purpose.

Rather than battling with ourselves over unmet goals, wrestling with what others say or do, or allowing negativity to consume us, we must focus on standing firm in faith. Trusting God and leaning on Him enables us to rise above the noise and distractions. The good fight of faith aligns us with God's plans and unlocks the blessings and victories He has in store.

So, keep fighting—with trust in God, persistent prayer, and unwavering belief in His promises. This fight isn't just about overcoming challenges; it's about growing into the person God created you to be and stepping into the destiny He has designed for you. Stand firm and fight faithfully—your victory is assured!

Week 37 Wednesday

God Will Defend Us!

"Then Nebuchadnezzar said, "Praise be to the God of Shadrach, Meshach and Abednego, who has sent his angel and rescued his servants!"
(Daniel 3:28, NIV)

It is truly incredible to reflect on the story of the three teenage Hebrew boys, Shadrach, Meshach, and Abednego, and how the king openly acknowledged that their God was the true God. This same king, in his pride and authority, had ordered these boys to be thrown into the fiery furnace as punishment for refusing to bow down to his golden idol. He knew the fiery furnace was a place of immediate death—it had already claimed the lives of others—but these young men emerged completely unharmed, untouched by the flames.

The king witnessed a miracle that could not be denied, and his heart was moved to recognize the power of the God who protected them. What stands out about Shadrach, Meshach, and Abednego is their unwavering faith. They refused to compromise their beliefs or conform to the demands of the king. Without trying to convince or argue with anyone, their actions and faith spoke louder than any words could.

The same God who defended these boys stands ready to defend us in our own challenges. We don't need to prove to anyone who we believe in or what He can do. Like them, we must stand firm in our faith, trusting God completely and refusing to give up. He is faithful and will always come to our defense. His power is limitless, and He will deliver us just as He delivered them. Stand strong, knowing that God fights for you!

Week 37 Thursday

Pleasure In Prospering!

"Let them say continually, "Let the LORD be magnified, who has pleasure in the prosperity of His servant." (Psalm 35:27, NKJV)

We are encouraged to train our minds to embrace and repeat this powerful declaration: *"Let God be magnified who takes pleasure in prospering me."* Often, our thoughts drift toward lack—what we don't have, what others should be doing, or what we feel is missing. This mindset can overshadow the truth of what we already have in God. Ego, insecurities, and a lack of confidence can sometimes block us from fully appreciating who God is and the incredible things He can do for us.

By consistently speaking and affirming this declaration, we form a habit that strengthens our faith and builds spiritual muscles. When we remind ourselves that God takes pleasure in prospering us, it shifts our focus from limitation to possibility. It reinforces the truth that we are not failures but individuals created to thrive, grow, and prosper through His blessings.

This practice isn't just about positive thinking—it's about aligning our hearts and minds with the truth of God's promises. Write it down, keep it in a visible place, and declare it daily: *"Let God be magnified who takes pleasure in prospering me."* Over time, this affirmation will become a deeply rooted belief, fueling your faith and confidence in His plans.

In all you do, trust that God will make it fruitful. His pleasure is found in your success, joy, and prosperity. Speak it, believe it, and watch His blessings unfold in your life. You were created to prosper!

Week 37 Friday

Birthing Seeds Of Greatness!

Those who sow in tears shall reap with shouts of joy." (Psalms 126:5, ESV).

So many families today struggle with broken relationships, leaving children and parents at odds with one another. Dysfunction has become all too common, making us yearn for a world where every family is united, full of love and harmony. Have you ever wondered why Pharaoh sought to kill all the babies or why Herod followed the same path? The enemy's goal was to destroy the seed—the potential and greatness that God places within families. He recognizes that your children, your relationships, and your family have seeds of greatness that can outgrow and overshadow his influence in the garden of this world.

For those who serve the Lord, these seeds carry incredible potential. This is why we must protect our hearts and homes, standing guard against the enemy's strategies that aim to destroy what God has planted in us. When we cry, our tears become water for these seeds. They nurture and nourish the greatness within our children, our marriages, and our relationships.

When was the last time you shed tears of prayer over your family? The scripture teaches us that those who sow in tears will reap with shouts of joy. Your tears are not wasted—they are watering the seeds of God's promises and preparing the harvest to come.

Hold onto hope and keep sowing in faith, even through the struggles. God sees every tear and promises that joy will follow. Protect the seeds of greatness in your life and trust in His plan!

Week 38 Monday

Protect Yourself!

"Oh, the joys of those who do not follow the advice of the wicked, or stand around with sinners, or join in with mockers."
(Psalm 1:1, NLT)

Over the past few years, we've had the joy of meeting incredible people from Canada, the USA, Europe, the Caribbean, and South America. Some of these connections felt so natural, as if we had known them our whole lives. They bring immense joy, and conversations flow effortlessly, often lasting for hours. These are the kinds of people we should surround ourselves with—those who add value to our lives, actively listen, and engage without allowing ego, insecurities, or self-doubt to interfere. They inspire and uplift us.

On the other hand, people who focus on impressing others, dominate conversations, or believe they are always right can cloud our lives and weigh down our spirits. Their negativity, constant criticism, and need to control can poison the atmosphere around us. Scripture warns against such individuals, calling them wicked and cautioning us to avoid their unwise counsel. Spending time with those lacking confidence in God or those who mock and belittle others can lead us away from His path.

Instead, invest your time with Christ-centered individuals who reflect God's love. These are the people who encourage, uplift, and help you become the best version of yourself. Their words and actions will nurture your faith and inspire you to grow. Surround yourself with those who align with God's principles and bring light into your life. Choose relationships that enrich your journey and lead you closer to Him. You deserve to flourish in a positive, God-focused environment!

Week 38 Tuesday

Source of Your Resource

"See what great love the Father has lavished on us, that we should be called children of God! And that is what we are!" (1 John 3:1, NIV)

It's a profound honor to be called part of royalty and to be a friend of someone so powerful, fearless, and infinite in resources—the Creator who owns the cattle on a thousand hills and rules over the universe. He is never lacking, never hesitant to extend His hand when we need Him most. Everything in creation submits to His authority, and yet, He has chosen us to be His friends and adopted us as His children into His kingdom. What an extraordinary privilege!

With God as the source of all our resources, there is no limit to what we can accomplish. Never believe the lies that you're not smart enough, not capable enough, or that your dreams are unattainable. Those thoughts only rob you of the truth: God fully supports you in fulfilling the desires He has placed within your heart. His plans for you are greater than you can imagine.

You are far more significant and capable than you may realize. What seems beyond reach is fully within God's ability to bring to fruition. Trust in Him, and step forward with faith. As a child of the One who created all things, you hold the power to achieve greatness. Let His assurance guide you and watch Him turn impossibilities into miraculous realities. You are chosen, loved, and destined for incredible things! Walk confidently in the knowledge of who you are—a cherished child of the King.

Week 38 Wednesday

Approved By God!

"Am I now trying to win the approval of human beings, or of God? Or am I trying to please people? If I were still trying to please people, I would not be a servant of Christ." (Galatians 1:10, NIV)

Many of us live life as if we're on a treadmill—constantly moving, striving to prove ourselves, and seeking approval from others. In the process, we often discredit our own worth by placing the demands of others above our well-being, tirelessly going above and beyond. This cycle can lead to burnout, leaving us feeling alone and unfulfilled. Even in the days of the early disciples, this issue was recognized and addressed.

We don't need the approval of others because we already have God's approval. He has declared us His masterpiece, uniquely created and chosen. Codependency or a need for external validation will never help us fulfill the plans God has set for us; instead, it will limit us. God calls us to be our best, relying solely on His approval and grace.

It's vital to reflect on whether we're seeking the approval of people or God. Are our actions motivated by pleasing others, or by serving Him? Scripture reminds us that if we focus on pleasing people, we cannot fully serve Christ. While loyalty and honor are important, they shouldn't be confused with dependency on external validation.

God has already approved and equipped you with all you need to succeed. His validation is enough, and His plans for you are greater than human limitations. Walk confidently in the knowledge that you are loved and chosen by God. He sees you, approves of you, and empowers you to accomplish all He has set before you!

Week 38 Thursday

Keep Travelling Steadily!

"Don't be impatient for the Lord to act! Keep travelling steadily along his pathway, and in due season, he will honour you with every blessing."
(Psalm 37:34, TLB)

In today's world, it often feels like there's a constant rush to meet endless demands. We've become so conditioned to live at full speed—always going, always doing, always accomplishing. With drive-thru banks, fast food, grocery pick-up services, doorstep deliveries, and the ability to order anything with just a tap, we've built a culture of instant gratification. Waiting feels like a burden, and impatience often becomes our default.

Yet, God's timing is beautifully different. His plans are never rushed, because He knows exactly when we'll be ready to receive what we ask for. While we wait, He doesn't leave us in silence or doubt; instead, He offers gentle reminders that He has not forgotten us. His delays are not denials—they are opportunities to grow, prepare, and align ourselves with His perfect will.

Scripture encourages us to avoid impatience as we wait for the Lord to act. Instead, we are called to stay on His path, traveling steadily and faithfully. The journey may feel long at times, but in due season, God promises to honor us with His abundant blessings. He sees your efforts, your faith, and your trust.

Let's commit to walking in God's pathway, trusting His timing and His plans. Keep your heart focused on His promises and continue traveling forward, step by step. When His perfect moment comes, every blessing He has prepared will unfold in ways more beautiful than you can imagine. His timing is worth the wait!

Week 38 Friday

Unexpected Rewards!

"I will restore to you the years that the swarming locust has eaten, the hopper, the destroyer, and the cutter, my great army, which I sent among you."
(Joel 2:25, ESV)

Life often presents moments of loss, whether it's stolen opportunities, broken promises, health struggles, or time slipping away unfairly. Some have faced unjust dismissals from work, missed promotions despite their qualifications, or deep disappointments caused by others' actions. Yet, no matter the challenges or the enemy's attempts to steal our joy, God assures us of His promise to restore. He works in ways that bring unexpected blessings and rewards beyond our imagination.

God has a mighty army tirelessly working on our behalf, ensuring restoration for all that seems lost. The years we believe have been taken from us are not gone forever—He is able to propel blessings into the present. Doors that were once closed are being opened. New opportunities, meaningful connections, and unexpected favors are being prepared for us. His restoration is powerful, transforming even the most painful losses into seasons of abundance.

It's important not to let the past define who we are or restrict what we're capable of achieving. The mistakes, disappointments, and hardships do not hold authority over our future. Instead, God calls us to release the past and embrace the future He has designed for us—a future filled with success, hope, and fulfillment.

Trust in His ability to renew, rebuild, and restore. By keeping our hearts open to His plan and stepping forward in faith, we will see His promises unfold in remarkable ways. Let go of the past and confidently step into the brighter days ahead!

Week 39 Monday
God Will Take A Bullet

"And we know that all things work together for good to those who love God, to those who are the called according to His purpose."(Romans 8:28, NKJV)

Life can feel overwhelming when it seems like the world is turning upside-down, especially during times when we face unfavorable circumstances. Whether it's receiving negative news from a doctor or experiencing job termination from a boss, these moments can be deeply discouraging. It's important to remind ourselves that the challenges we face stem from the brokenness in this world caused by sin. The enemy's goal is to distract and destroy the destiny God has lovingly designed for us.

In these moments of struggle, we are called to immerse ourselves in the presence of God. By developing a close and intimate relationship with Him, we find protection, comfort, and strength. God's love surrounds us, giving us hope even in the darkest of times. Don't allow discouragement to overwhelm your heart—every trial can be an opportunity to draw closer to Him.

Though some may feel upset or angry with God in moments of pain, choosing to love Him even more allows us to experience His embrace. The closer we are to God, the harder it is for the enemy to touch us. Just as a father would shield his children and take a bullet to protect them, so does God for us. His love is unyielding, and His protection is steadfast.

Through every storm, hold tightly to God's promises. Trust in His unwavering love and let your relationship with Him empower you to face life's difficulties with courage and peace. God will always stand in defense of His beloved children!

Week 39 Tuesday

Not Cease To Bear Fruits!

"He is like a tree planted by water, that sends out its roots by the stream, and does not fear when heat comes, for its leaves remain green, and is not anxious in the year of drought, for it does not cease to bear fruit."
(Jeremiah 17:8, ESV)

God beautifully compares us to a tree planted by a stream, unaffected by drought or scorching heat. This tree continues to thrive and produce because its roots draw nourishment from the living water. Similarly, we are called to stay connected to God, who is our endless source of nourishment and strength. He sustains us, enabling us to grow and fulfill the purpose set before us, regardless of the challenges we face.

As we remain rooted in His presence, we can outlast opposition and stand firm in faith. We are not defined by the hardships we see in the natural world but by the truth and promises revealed in the supernatural. Trusting in God's provision allows us to rise above the anxieties and limitations that try to hold us back.

Never stop believing in the best. God will provide for every need and equip you to thrive. It's essential to separate yourself from negative environments, toxic relationships, and habits that may hinder your growth. By stepping away from anything that limits your potential, you open yourself up to His abundant blessings and the opportunity to produce your very best.

With God as your source, you are resilient, fruitful, and empowered. Let your roots deepen in His living water, and you will flourish in ways beyond imagination. We will not cease to bear fruit, for His nourishment gives us strength to keep growing, thriving, and fulfilling His divine purpose!

Week 39 Wednesday

Be Infused With God!

"Never turn your gaze from me, for I am your faithful God. I will infuse you with my strength and help you in every situation. I will hold you firmly with my victorious right hand." (Isaiah 41:10 TPT)

Life can feel overwhelming at times—burnout, exhaustion, stress, and weariness can weigh us down, leaving us feeling like it's all too much to handle. The constant demands placed on us can drain the joy and purpose that God created for us to experience. Yet, even in these moments of struggle, we are reminded through scripture of God's incredible empowerment and divine resilience. His strength is greater than any challenge we face and surpasses all the pressures of this world that try to steal our peace and happiness.

We are encouraged to keep our eyes fixed on God, never turning away from Him, even when life feels unbearable. He is a faithful and unwavering God who promises to uphold us with His victorious right hand. In every situation, He will infuse us with His strength, soaking us in His power and grace, so we can face life's challenges with courage and determination.

No matter how heavy the burden feels, God's presence offers renewal and hope. When we choose to refocus on Him, we are reminded that we are not alone. His love and faithfulness will guide us and provide the strength we need to press on.

Take a moment to pause and reconnect with God today. Allow His presence to surround you, renew your spirit, and fill you with the resilience only He can provide. Let Him remind you that, through Him, you are equipped to overcome every obstacle with peace and assurance.

Week 39 Thursday

God Will Turn Things

"The king's heart is in the hand of the LORD, like the rivers of water; He turns it wherever He wishes." (Proverbs 21:1, NKJV)

What a beautiful reminder of the depth of God's love and power! Scripture tells us that people's hearts are in the hands of the Lord, and like rivers of water, He can turn them wherever He desires. God has the ability to change the hearts of those who may stand against us and make them work in our favor. He can direct their thoughts, give them dreams, and show them what needs to be done on our behalf.

At the appointed time, God will move in ways we cannot predict. Those who said "no," who believed "it can't happen," or dismissed things as "impossible" will be realigned by God's divine plan. No obstacle is too great to prevent His purpose from coming to pass. What God has planned for our destiny will surely be fulfilled.

Instead of focusing on the challenges before us, we are called to seek God's heart and trust His timing. Nothing in our lives is set in stone—everything is subject to His divine intervention. Situations that seem overwhelming or permanent are often just distractions meant to discourage us.

When we have done all we can, it's time to release our worries to Him. Trust that God will turn circumstances and even hearts to meet our needs, like rivers flowing in their appointed direction. Let go of the stress and place your faith in His hands. Trust God today and watch His plans unfold!

Week 39 Friday
Your Enemy Will Let Go!

"Pharaoh said, "Who is the LORD, that I should obey him and let Israel go? I do not know the LORD, and I will not let Israel go." (Exodus 5:2, NIV)

The Israelites endured harsh slavery under Pharaoh, but God instructed Moses to demand their release, saying, "Let My people go." Though the task was daunting, Moses obeyed, even when Pharaoh stubbornly refused. Scripture captures Pharaoh's defiance: "Who is the LORD, that I should obey Him and let Israel go? I do not know the LORD, and I will not let Israel go." This refusal reminds us that the enemy will resist releasing the freedom and blessings meant for us. He fights to keep us bound, holding onto what we know rightfully belongs to us.

Even when we hear God's promises and yet see no immediate results, we must remember that the enemy is relentless in his attempts to block God's plans. Discouragement may tempt us to give up, but persistence is key. Just as Moses continued returning to Pharaoh, reminding him of God's command, we too must remain steadfast, trusting in God's promise and pushing forward despite resistance.

Moses's unwavering faith and persistence have inspired generations. Had he given up, the story of Israel's liberation might have been very different. Instead, his determination ultimately led to freedom as Pharaoh was compelled to let the Israelites go.

Let this story encourage you—remain steadfast in your faith and persistence. Your enemy will not hold on forever. Trust in God's plan, push forward, and know that what He has promised will come to pass. Freedom and blessings are on the horizon!

Week 40 Monday

God Does Not Disqualify Us!

"Now bring your brother Aaron near, and his sons with him from among the sons of Israel, so that he may serve as priest to Me." (Exodus 28:1, AMP))

Moses ascended Mount Sinai, where he spent 40 days and nights receiving the Ten Commandments from God. During his absence, his brother Aaron was left in charge of the Israelites. As the days stretched on, the people grew restless and demanded that Aaron create gods for them to worship. Under pressure, Aaron gave in and fashioned a golden calf for them. Despite knowing God's power and faithfulness—having witnessed His miracles and declared His words before Pharaoh—Aaron compromised and participated in a grave sin.

Yet, even in this failure, God did not abandon Aaron or write him off. Instead, God extended grace and still chose Aaron to become the first high priest of Israel. This demonstrates God's incredible mercy and willingness to restore us, even when we falter.

Like Aaron, we may stumble and fail, but we should not cancel ourselves or believe that God has disqualified us. His love remains steadfast, and He continues to see our worth and potential. While God's grace lifts us up, it also calls us to learn, grow, and choose a better path moving forward.

No matter how far you feel you've strayed, stand firm, accept God's embrace, and realign your heart with His. Allow His mercy to guide you back on track, and let His love remind you that your journey is far from over. With God, there is always the opportunity for renewal and purpose. Step forward with confidence in His grace!

Week 40 Tuesday

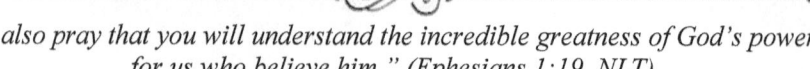
Only Believe!

"I also pray that you will understand the incredible greatness of God's power for us who believe him." (Ephesians 1:19, NLT)

In 1985, my uncle planted a seed of hope in my heart, promising to sponsor me if I came to Canada. He spoke of the opportunities to change my life and the lives of my parents. By 1987, the doors seemed to open, but he never followed through on his promise. Left with no other choice, I placed my trust in the God I knew, believing He would guide me to become a Canadian. True to His faithfulness, God directed my steps, leading me to a drywall taper who played a key role in my sponsorship. For three long years, I held on to my faith, and eventually, I became a Canadian resident.

Today, I am living proof of what it means to believe in the God who never fails to fulfill His word. He has given us an extraordinary gift—the ability to believe. Paul, the apostle, prayed that we would grasp the incredible greatness of God's power, which is available to those who choose to believe in Him.

No matter the challenges or delays, we must never lose our ability to believe. In Mark 9:23, Jesus reminds us, "Everything is possible for one who believes." Let this truth inspire you to hold firm in faith, no matter the circumstances. Never stop believing in God's promises. He will never give up on you, and His plans for your life will come to fruition in His perfect timing!

Week 40 Wednesday

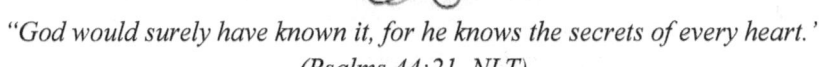

"God would surely have known it, for he knows the secrets of every heart."
(Psalms 44:21, NLT)

Some of us may not always realize the depth of God's understanding of the heart. He knows what others think about us, how they act toward us, and even how we respond to those actions. God also sees the enemy's plans and knows how to use them to work for us rather than against us. Beyond this, He understands our weaknesses and flaws, anticipating how we might react in moments of challenge.

It's important for us to be honest with ourselves, recognizing our shortcomings and flaws with humility. When we fail to reflect on the condition of our hearts—how we think about ourselves and others—we unintentionally invite emotional struggles into our lives. While God will never turn His back on us, we risk making life more difficult when our hearts are not aligned with Him. His steadfast love remains, but we create roadblocks when we neglect the state of our inner self.

God knows every secret held within our hearts. We may be able to hide our thoughts from others, but we can never hide them from Him. That's why transparency with God is crucial. Only through His power can we overcome our enemies. Only in His name can we rise above our weaknesses and flaws.

Align your heart with Him today. Let His love and grace guide you, so that when God searches your heart, He finds it in harmony with His expectations. There is peace and strength in surrendering to His power.

Week 40 Thursday
All His Promises!

"So don't ever be afraid, dearest friends! Your loving Father joyously gives you his kingdom with all its promises!" (Luke 12:32, TPT)

Life often brings challenges that can feel overwhelming, some more intense than others. Yet, in the midst of our struggles, we hold onto the truth that God is faithful. He heals, provides, delivers, protects, and completely turns situations around in ways beyond our understanding. Despite this assurance, our minds can still wander to lies—lies we hear from others or lies born within our own thoughts. These doubts and fears creep in, stealing our peace and robbing us of restful sleep, sometimes making us feel like our own minds are working against us.

It's in these moments that we need to realign our thoughts with God's truth, using His Word as our foundation. When we redirect our hearts and minds to reflect His perspective, we cancel the power of doubt, fear, and deception. God has given us His promises, and through Him, we will overcome every challenge we face.

Scripture tells us not to be afraid, reminding us of the loving Father who has joyfully given us His kingdom with all its promises. His power is limitless, and His love for us is steadfast. He is able to bring us through our circumstances in ways we cannot imagine.

Let's refocus on God and trust in His faithfulness. He has equipped us with the ability to rise above fear and doubt. Don't limit God's work in your life. Hold tightly to His promises and know He will guide you through to victory! He has given us every reason to believe.

Week 40 Friday

Know The Promises Of God!

"All of God's promises have their yes in him. That is why we say Amen through him to the glory of God." (2 Corinthians 1:20, *)*

We've all made promises that we couldn't keep due to life's unexpected twists and turns. Whether to ourselves, family, friends, or even God, these broken commitments remind us of our human limitations. Yet, there is one truth that remains unshaken—God always keeps His promises. He is steadfast and unwavering, no matter our circumstances or shortcomings. Even when we fail Him, turn away, or doubt His faithfulness, He remains true to His Word.

God's promises are not conditional upon our perfection. He places them in His Word to reveal His unchanging love and faithfulness. Through His promises, He is glorified, and we are reminded of His incredible grace. To fully receive what He has pledged, we must first understand what He offers—good health, prosperity, and the assurance that we are destined to rise above challenges. God calls us to be the head and not the tail, lenders and not borrowers. He invites us to ask, and it shall be given; to seek, and we shall find; to knock, and the doors will be opened. His promises ensure that we will never lack and that His provision will always sustain us.

Take time to reflect on His promises. Write them down, and bring them back to Him in prayer. Let God's faithfulness strengthen your hope and trust. He will honor every word He has spoken and lead you into the fullness of what He has planned for your life. Trust in His promises, for they are unbreakable!

Week 41 Monday
God Will Fight For Us!

"The LORD said to him, "I will be with you. And you will destroy the Midianites as if you were fighting against one man." (Judges 6:16, NLT)

When Gideon faced an army of 135,000 soldiers, God reduced his own troops to just three hundred. From Gideon's perspective, the situation must have seemed impossible—he was overwhelmingly outnumbered, and the odds appeared to spell the end of his life. Yet, God reassured him with a powerful promise: "I will be with you. And you will destroy the Midianites as if you were fighting against one man."

Even though God had the power to annihilate the Midianites on His own, Gideon was still required to lead his men into battle. Trusting in God's Word, Gideon attacked during the night, and something miraculous happened—the enemy was thrown into confusion and began to destroy one another. Without breaking a sweat, Gideon and his army watched victory unfold, all because they stepped out in faith and obeyed God's instructions.

Gideon's story is an incredible example of how we should respond to the challenges in our own lives. When adverse circumstances arise and anxiety begins to creep in, we are called to fix our eyes on God rather than our situations. As Gideon stepped forward in faith, we too must trust that when we step out, God will step in.

God's presence is our refuge, a secret place where He releases solutions to the obstacles we face. Instead of allowing fear and doubt to take hold, let's rely on His wisdom and power. Don't focus on the impossibilities—look unto God, knowing He will guide you through every challenge and lead you to victory!

Week 41 Tuesday

Leave It Up To God!

"Stop striving and know that I am God; I will be exalted among the nations, I will be exalted on the earth." (Psalm 46:10, NASB)

We often find ourselves guilty of trying to make everything happen—pushing to help others make the right choices, grow our businesses or careers, heal ourselves, and reach milestones we've set for our lives. In that pursuit, we may force open the wrong doors, mistakenly believing it's God's plan, and create unhealthy connections with the wrong people in an effort to bring our desires to life. While it's true that faith without works is dead, there's immense peace in fully depending on God.

The constant pressure we place on ourselves often leads to sleepless nights, overwhelmed thoughts, and mental exhaustion. Yet, scripture gently reminds us, "Stop striving and know that I am God…" To strive means to struggle or fight vigorously, or to make great efforts to achieve something. God invites us to step away from that struggle and rely on Him instead, trusting in His perfect timing. When we stop forcing ourselves into situations and surrender our stress to Him, we discover freedom and security in His faithfulness.

Whatever is weighing heavily on your heart today, bring it to the Lord. Allow Him to intervene and guide your path forward. God wants to be exalted in your life, and He uses our challenges as opportunities to show His power and glory. Trust in Him—His plans are always greater than we can imagine, and He will provide in ways that ease our burdens and fulfill His promises. Let go, and let God make it happen!

Week 41 Wednesday

God Is Madly In Love!

"No power in the sky above or in the earth below—indeed, nothing in all creation will ever be able to separate us from the love of God that is revealed in Christ Jesus our Lord." (Romans 8:39, NLT)

Many of us have felt the incredible power of love—a love so warm, comforting, and joyful that it seems to fill every corner of our hearts. Love can bring peace, happiness, and satisfaction. It's an emotion so powerful that it wins over even the hardest hearts. Yet, when love feels broken, the pain it leaves behind is one no earthly remedy can heal.

Scripture reminds us that there is nothing—absolutely nothing—that can separate us from the love of God. His love is unconditional, embracing us in all our imperfections. He isn't angry at us for our weaknesses, mistakes, or flaws. Instead, He loves us just as we are—deeply, unshakably, and endlessly. God's love is the antidote to our insecurities, the source of our confidence, and the key to overcoming low self-esteem.

We are called to fall so deeply in love with God, knowing He will never reject us. His love provides us with strength and stability, taking away our fears and replacing them with unshakable peace. Just as earthly parents would give their lives for their children, God does so much more for His own. His love is infinitely greater, sheltering and protecting us in every way.

Take a moment today to truly embrace the love of God. Let it wrap around you, healing your heart and restoring your spirit. When you welcome His love, you'll discover a joy and peace unlike any other. Trust in Him, and see how His love transforms your life!

Week 41 Thursday

Get Out Of Your Boat!

""Come," he said. Then Peter got down out of the boat, walked on the water and came toward Jesus." (Matthew 14:29, NIV)

After feeding over five thousand men, not counting women and children, Jesus went to pray, while His disciples sailed into deep waters, finding themselves "in the middle of the sea." As the boat was tossed by waves due to the strong wind, they saw Jesus walking toward them on the water. Mistaking Him for a ghost, fear gripped their hearts. Amid the storm, Peter stepped out of the boat and began walking on the water toward Jesus. However, when he focused on the boisterous wind, fear overtook him, and he started to sink. In desperation, Peter cried out, "Lord, save me," and Jesus immediately reached out His hand, rescuing him.

This powerful story reminds us of the importance of stepping out in faith, especially during life's storms. When we face challenges that feel overwhelming, it's easy to focus on the "waves" around us—the fears, doubts, and difficulties that threaten to pull us under. Yet, Jesus calls us to trust Him, to depend on His Spirit, and to know that He will always reach out to save us.

Walking on water symbolizes a profound reliance on the Spirit of God. He is our Helper, sustaining us and ensuring we don't sink under the weight of life's pressures. Just as Peter took a leap of faith, we are invited to step out of our comfort zones and trust in His divine guidance. Get out of your boat today and experience the power of God's steadfast love and protection!

Week 41 Friday

Get Out Your Tent!

"And He brought him outside [his tent into the starlight] and said, Look now toward the heavens and count the stars—if you are able to number them. Then He said to him, So shall your descendants be." (Genesis 15:5, AMPC)

It's fascinating how the stars reveal themselves in the dark, a reminder of the beauty that can only be seen when we step outside our comfort zones. When God took Abraham out of his tent, the world around him was silent—no electricity, no friends, no family, no distractions. Just Abraham and God in the stillness of the night. God asked Abraham, "Look now toward the heavens and count the stars…. So shall your descendants be." At 75 years old, Abraham received a vision from God, one that promised a destiny far greater than he could imagine.

This story teaches us something profound: as long as we remain in our tents, shielding ourselves from the unknown, we won't be able to see the incredible plans God has for us. Inside, we may only see the people and things we're accustomed to, but outside—beyond our fears and comfort—lies a destiny full of favor, success, and purpose.

Age is never a limitation for God's vision. Whether young or old, His plans for us are filled with joy and prosperity. To step into His promises, we must be willing to venture out of our tents, even if the darkness feels unsettling or lonely. It's often in these quiet, still moments that God speaks, revealing His path for our lives.

Trust His guidance, embrace His vision, and take that step into the unknown. God's plans for your destiny are far greater than you can imagine! Step out and let Him lead.

Week 42 Monday

Give Yourself A Chance!

"Your faithfulness extends to every generation, like the earth you created; it endures by your decree, for everything serves your plans."
(Psalm 119:91, TLB)

Many of us have experienced moments where life feels stagnant—waiting for a financial breakthrough, navigating struggles in relationships, or searching for clarity on God's plan. These seasons can feel overwhelming, filled with disappointment after disappointment, leaving us unsure about the next step forward. Yet, even in the midst of uncertainty, God is at work, aligning our lives to walk in His favor.

God's faithfulness assures us that He will do whatever it takes to lead us toward the breakthrough we've been praying for. He will connect us with the right people, inspire us with ideas, and plant dreams and visions in our hearts. His desire is for us to step into a destiny filled with purpose, joy, and success. God will create opportunities and open doors that move us closer to fulfilling the life He designed for us.

Scripture reminds us that everything serves His plans, and His ultimate goal is for us to prosper and be in good health. We are called to trust in His timing, remain open, and embrace the blessings He has prepared for us. When we give ourselves a chance to lean into His guidance, we can uncover paths we never imagined possible.

Don't allow discouragement to hold you back or keep you from stepping into the opportunities God has placed before you. Be open-hearted, trust His plans, and let Him lead you to the next chapter of your life. The breakthrough you've been waiting for is closer than you think!

Week 42 Tuesday
Get Out Of The Mud!

"The steps of a good man are ordered by the LORD, and He delights in his way." (Psalm 37:23, NKJV)

In life, we're faced with choices about which steps to take, often shaped by our circumstances. At times, we've made impulsive decisions that later brought regret, reminding us of the importance of intentional living. Scripture encourages us to first focus on being good men and women—living a godly life that pleases Him. This means embracing righteous living, cultivating the character of God, demonstrating the fruits of the Spirit, and maintaining a positive and faith-filled attitude.

When we align our lives with God's desires, we position ourselves to achieve our goals and see our dreams fulfilled. God doesn't want us to merely exist—He wants us to enjoy each precious second of life on this earth. Though hiccups, roadblocks, and challenges will inevitably come our way, a life that honors Him brings protection and purpose.

And even when we find ourselves stuck in the "mud of life," weighed down by difficulties, God doesn't leave us there. He gives us the strength and wisdom to stand, navigate the challenges, and emerge stronger. His guidance provides a path toward victory, reminding us that we are never alone in the journey.

Follow the steps that God orders for your life. Trust His direction and embrace the victories that come from walking in faith. He has extraordinary plans for you, and with Him, every step becomes purposeful!

Week 42 Wednesday

 Take The Limits Off!

"I can do all things through him who strengthens me."
(Philippians 4:13, NKJV)

Not many of us ever imagined ourselves juggling all the roles we now embrace—being career-oriented, educated, managing time, parenting, fostering strong relationships, socializing, enjoying hobbies, playing musical instruments, speaking new languages, traveling, and impacting lives. Yet, here we are, accomplishing these extraordinary feats because our Creator has equipped us with the ability to do anything we set our minds to. We hold within us the potential to climb the highest mountains and swim the deepest oceans if only we choose to believe in what we're capable of achieving.

It's time to remove the limits we place on ourselves. Instead of fixating on the obstacles standing before us, let's shift our focus to the possibilities. Scripture reminds us of a powerful truth: we can do all things through Jesus, who strengthens us. There are no boundaries to what we can achieve with His guidance. He will align us with the right people and resources to bring our goals and dreams to life.

Don't let your thoughts or feelings dictate your abilities or define your future. God's promises encourage us to persevere, knowing that His strength is always with us. Embrace the opportunities before you and trust that He will pave the way for your success. With faith and determination, there is nothing you cannot accomplish. Step forward confidently, and let His power move through you as you reach new heights. You are limitless through His grace!

Week 42 Thursday

Find The King In You!

"Now why do you cry aloud? Is there no king in you?" (Micah 4:9, ESV)

This passage reflects a pivotal moment in history when an invading army killed Israel's king, leaving the nation without leadership for the first time. The Israelites were devastated, lost, and unsure of how to move forward—feeling like "fish out of water." In the midst of their despair, the prophet Micah spoke these powerful words: "Now, why do you cry aloud? Is there no king in you?" These words were a reminder of the divine strength and royalty God had placed within them.

Just as Micah encouraged the Israelites, we too need to remind ourselves that there is a king living inside of us. We are not a mistake; we were purposefully created with inherent value, worth, and qualities of royalty that are waiting to be released. God has placed within us the ability to speak with authority, wisdom, and humility, making decisions that honor Him and positively impact others.

God brings people into our lives for a reason. Embrace those connections and allow them to help you grow into the person He designed you to be. Living in freedom and victory begins with recognizing the "king" within us and trusting in the royal qualities God has given us.

Step into your identity with confidence, knowing that God has equipped you for greatness. Speak boldly, make decisions wisely, and let God's purpose shine through you. You are called to live in victory, empowered by the presence of the King within you!

Week 42 Friday

Avoid Mental Detached

"About midnight Paul and Silas were praying and singing hymns to God, and the other prisoners were listening to them." (Acts 16:25, NIV)

Paul and Silas found themselves in prison, beaten and bruised for sharing the gospel. They were undoubtedly in pain—both physically and emotionally—and likely struggling with exhaustion. Yet, even in their darkest moments, they didn't allow worry, anger, or disappointment to take hold. Instead of questioning God or feeling ashamed, they chose to lift their voices in praise. As they prayed and sang hymns to God, the Bible recounts that "about midnight, Paul and Silas were praying and singing hymns to God, and the other prisoners were listening to them."

Their unwavering faith is a powerful reminder for us today. Life often throws us into situations that challenge our faith, leaving us frustrated or even tempted to disconnect from God. But just like Paul and Silas, we are called to stand firm in the face of adversity. When difficulties arise, don't allow the enemy to steal your connection to God. Instead, confront the challenges with prayer and praise, declaring God's goodness regardless of the circumstances.

Disconnecting from God can lead us down paths of confusion and discouragement, but embracing Him keeps us grounded and moving forward. Spend time in His presence today, pouring out your heart in prayer and lifting Him up in praise. Let others around you witness your faith and find inspiration in your steadfast devotion. God is always with us, even in the storm, and He will bring us through every trial. Praise Him boldly and trust in His unfailing love!

Week 43 Monday

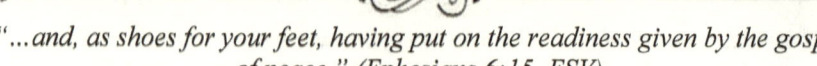 Wearing God's Shoe!

"...and, as shoes for your feet, having put on the readiness given by the gospel of peace." (Ephesians 6:15, ESV)

Scripture beautifully urges us to put on the armor of God, and it's fascinating that the shoes in this armor symbolize peace. When we walk in God's shoes, we are walking in calmness and assurance. Peace is something the whole world craves—it's a universal longing that can only be fully realized through the gospel. Could it be that God understands the challenges and difficulties we'll face in life and has gifted us these shoes to help us walk calmly and peacefully through it all?

God's desire is never for us to live in fear, lose hope, or be consumed with worry. He does not want anxiety to overwhelm or cripple our minds. Instead, He equips us with His strength and provides divine strategies to navigate even the toughest circumstances. Through His grace, we possess spiritual resilience—the ability to rise above feelings of defeat and stand firm in faith, anchored by His peace.

No matter what situation you find yourself in, God's peace is always available. It's found in His presence, where your heart can rest from fear and worry. His shoes of peace are a reminder that He is with you, guiding your steps every day.

Make the choice to wear His shoes, and let peace lead the way. Walk boldly through life, trusting in His promises and His unfailing love. His peace will sustain you, no matter the obstacles you face!

Week 43 Tuesday

Difficult Situations!

"But He said, "The things that are impossible with people are possible with God." (Luke 18:27, NKJV)

God has a remarkable way of working through the most challenging circumstances. Consider the stories of how He empowered a young boy to defeat Goliath, gave a child to a couple at one hundred years old, and called a backslider to speak to the people of Nineveh. He blessed a barren woman with a child and chose a virgin to bring His Son into the world. He commanded a blind man to wash at a pool and restored his sight. He raised a dead man to life and multiplied three fish and five loaves to feed thousands. Each of these impossible situations became a testimony of His presence and power.

The greater the challenge, the more profoundly God's glory is revealed. Our struggles—whether they involve finances, relationships, physical or mental health, parenting, marriage, or work—draw His attention. No matter the difficulty, His power transforms impossibilities into possibilities. Scripture reminds us, "The things that are impossible with people are possible with God." This truth assures us that no obstacle is beyond His reach.

When faced with challenges, bring them to God. Trust in His ability to work wonders where solutions seem unattainable. Lean on His promises and watch His extraordinary plans unfold. Whatever may feel overwhelming today, place it in His hands and allow His presence to shine through. With God, every challenge becomes an opportunity for a breakthrough. Give it to Him, and witness His work!

Week 43 Wednesday
God Will Make A Way!

"Behold, I will do a new thing, now it shall spring forth; shall you not know it? I will even make a road in the wilderness and rivers in the desert." (Isaiah 43:19, NKJV)

God's words to the children of Israel were full of hope and reassurance. He promised to make a road through the wilderness and rivers in the desert, ensuring they would never go thirsty and their animals—valuable assets to their survival—would be cared for. The Israelites, held captive in Babylon and facing the harsh realities of the desert, felt uncertain about their journey home. But God comforted them, revealing that He has no secrets. He shared His plans openly, assuring them of His divine provision.

This same promise applies to us today. God doesn't keep secrets from His children. When we feel stuck in our own "desert" moments, unsure of which direction to take, He is there to guide us. He will create pathways through the obstacles, bring refreshment to our weary souls, and ensure our needs and resources are protected. Just as He revealed His plans to the Israelites, God will reveal His blueprint for our lives, allowing us to trust in His wisdom and find confidence in His timing.

No matter how overwhelming your circumstances may seem, you are never helpless. God will not leave you to navigate life's challenges alone. His guidance is steadfast, and His love is constant. Trust in Him today, even in your desert moments, and watch as He makes a way where none seems possible. His plans for you are filled with hope, renewal, and purpose. Lean into His presence and let Him lead you forward!

Week 43 Thursday

Seeds Of Greatness!

"You are the light of the world." (Matthew 5:14, NIV)

Jesus spoke these powerful words to His disciples—ordinary people just like us. Among them were fishermen, a tax collector, and even a zealot, someone passionate and uncompromising in their ideals. Yet, Jesus called them the light of the world. Imagine how those around them might have reacted. Would they have believed these humble individuals could bring light to the world? Jesus, however, saw greatness within them—potential that would shine brightly and make a profound impact.

The same is true for you. God sees the seeds of greatness He has planted in your life. He recognizes what you're capable of, even when you may not see it yourself. His vision for you is one of purpose, influence, and blessing. Like the disciples, you have the power to be a light in the lives of others, spreading His love and making a meaningful difference.

To bring these seeds of greatness to life, we must speak to ourselves with faith and nurture them through God's strength. Scripture reminds us that we can do all things through Christ who strengthens us. He equips us to overcome challenges, serve others, and fulfill the unique purpose He's given each of us.

Take time to recognize the potential God sees in you. Water those seeds with prayer, encouragement, and acts of faith, and watch as they grow into something extraordinary. You are destined to shine—embrace the greatness within you and let it flourish!

Week 43 Friday

Don't Get Distracted!

"So the chief priests made plans to kill Lazarus as well, for on account of him many of the Jews were going over to Jesus and believing in him."
(John 12:10–11, NIV)

This scripture recounts the incredible miracle of Jesus raising Lazarus from the dead—a moment no one could deny. Imagine the growing crowd of witnesses, eager to hear the details and see Lazarus, a man who had once been in the grave, now walking among them. Both Jesus and Lazarus gained immense popularity, like the release of a hit song or blockbuster movie. People were fascinated by this miraculous event, their curiosity drawing them closer.

Yet, not everyone celebrated this miracle. The chief priests, disturbed by Jesus and Lazarus's growing influence, plotted against them, seeking to take their lives. But despite their schemes, their plans did not succeed. God's purpose prevailed, proving that what He sets in motion cannot be undone.

When God begins to work in your life and your fruitfulness becomes visible, it's inevitable that others may respond with jealousy, envy, or opposition. Criticism and attempts to tear you down may come your way, but take heart. What God has planned for your destiny cannot be destroyed by human efforts or negativity.

Remain steadfast in your faith and stay close to His presence. Don't allow the voices of opposition or criticism to distract you from your purpose. Trust in God's protection and continue walking boldly in His plan for your life. As He did for Lazarus and Jesus, He will shield you and bring forth His destiny for you, no matter the challenges. His promises for your life are unshakable!

Week 44 Monday

Created To Produce!

"He shall be like a tree Planted by the rivers of water, That brings forth its fruit in its season, Whose leaf shall not wither; And whatever he does shall prosper." (Psalms 1:3, NKJV)

Trees, like all living things, need water to thrive. When nourished, trees are green, fruitful, and multiply effortlessly. Scripture draws a beautiful comparison, likening us to trees planted by rivers of water. Such trees bring forth fruit in their season, and their leaves never wither. Now, picture yourself as one of these trees.

When we root ourselves by rivers—immersed in the Word of God, prayer, worship, fellowship with others in faith, sharing the gospel, and engaging in mission work—we flourish. Our "leaves" stay vibrant, and we bear the fruits of our lives: skills, knowledge, wisdom, talents, and spiritual gifts. These fruits grow as we prosper in His presence.

As we grow, we'll see our lives becoming more fruitful and filled with purpose. God has designed each of us with the potential to thrive and make an impact. Stay connected to the right sources of nourishment and trust in His timing for your season.

Be intentional about where you're planted. Allow God's living water to refresh and sustain you. In time, you'll see yourself flourishing, bearing fruit, and fulfilling the purpose He has for your life. Stay rooted in Him and watch the harvest unfold!

Week 44 Tuesday

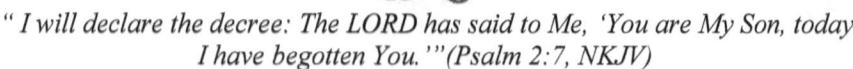
Prophesy Your Future!

" I will declare the decree: The LORD has said to Me, 'You are My Son, today I have begotten You.'"(Psalm 2:7, NKJV)

A decree is an official order issued by a legal authority—words spoken that carry the power to take effect. Scripture tells us that we have the authority to declare a decree, granted to us by God Himself. He governs our lives, empowering us to speak the desires of our hearts into existence. When we speak, our words carry weight, often inspiring action. Advice, suggestions, and recommendations we offer can influence and impact those who trust us.

God calls us to speak boldly, declaring decrees to the spiritual world from the abundance of our hearts. Through these declarations, we prophesy our own futures, trusting Him to align our paths with His perfect will. Imagine declaring: "I will be above and not beneath. I will be in good health and prosper. Goodness and mercy will follow me wherever I go. I will walk in favor, embraced by people in high places. I will be blessed in all I do, and my blessings will overflow to my children and their children, reaching a thousand generations."

This power to decree is a gift from God—a tool to shape your life according to His promises. Stand in faith and declare your decree today. Speak life over your circumstances and believe in the transformation God will bring. He has equipped you with this authority, and with it comes the ability to fulfill the incredible destiny He has designed for you. Embrace it, declare it, and watch His blessings unfold!

Week 44 Wednesday

God Will Make A Way!

"As soon as the priests who carry the ark of the LORD—the Lord of all the earth—set foot in the Jordan, its waters flowing downstream will be cut off and stand up in a heap." (Joshua 3:13, NIV)

Joshua and about two million Israelites stood before the Jordan River, which was flooding and appeared impassable. The river, likely about 45 meters wide, must have seemed overwhelming. As they looked at the powerful waters, many may have felt tempted to turn back, uncertain of how they could possibly cross. But Joshua spoke boldly to the priests carrying the Ark of the Lord and instructed them to keep moving forward. It was only when the priests stepped into the flooded river, getting their feet wet, that the waters miraculously parted, creating a path for the Israelites to cross safely.

If you were one of those priests, would you have had the courage to step into the river? Their faith and trust in God's promise made all the difference. This story is a profound reminder for us, especially when we face our own "flooding situations"—those moments in life when challenges feel insurmountable, and we see no way out except to give up or turn around.

But just as the priests carried the Ark of the Lord, we too carry the presence of God within us. The Lord of all the earth lives in us, and His power can open paths through even the most overwhelming circumstances. When you feel trapped or stuck, remember His presence in your life. Trust Him to guide you forward and make a way, even when it seems impossible. Let His strength lead the way and open doors you never thought possible. Step out in faith, knowing that with God, every obstacle can be overcome, and victory is always within reach. Trust Him today and see Him at work!

Week 44 Thursday

Spiritual Resiliency!

"We are pressed on every side by troubles, but we are not crushed. We are perplexed, but not driven to despair." (2 Corinthians 4:8, NLT)

This is exactly how many of us feel at times—the weight of life pressing down on us. Financial struggles, instability, overwhelming expectations, and endless demands can leave us feeling buried, much like a tiny seed beneath heavy soil. The weight may seem unbearable, hundreds or even thousands of times heavier than we can handle. But within every seed lies life, and God has placed that life within each of us.

When we feel overwhelmed, as though life has buried us under its pressures, we are not being destroyed—we are being planted. Scripture reassures us that though we are "pressed on every side by troubles, we are not crushed. We are perplexed, but not driven to despair." These moments are the beginning of a transformation, a season where we will germinate and burst forth into fruitfulness. God has instilled in us a supernatural resilience, equipping us to rise again with strength and endurance to face any storm.

Even Jesus experienced this. He was planted in the grave, and on the third day, He rose again in glory and victory. If He overcame, how much more can we rise through His power? The path has already been paved for us, and His strength is ours to lean on.

When the weight feels overwhelming, remember that you are not buried without purpose—you are planted with a promise. Trust in God's plan, knowing that this is a season of growth and renewal. In due time, you will rise stronger, bearing fruit and fulfilling the purpose He has designed for you. The best is yet to come!

Week 44 Friday

Have Confidence In God!

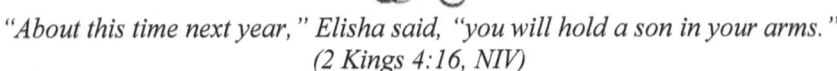

"About this time next year," Elisha said, "you will hold a son in your arms." (2 Kings 4:16, NIV)

This is the story of a woman who longed for a child but had given up hope, as her husband was old and their circumstances made it seem impossible. Then came Elisha, the prophet, who called her and spoke life-changing words as she stood in the doorway: "About this time next year, you shall embrace a son." Overwhelmed by the bold declaration, she replied, "No, my lord. Man of God, do not lie to your maidservant!" Yet, at the appointed time, just as Elisha had foretold, the woman conceived and gave birth to a son—a miracle that defied the limits of possibility.

This story reminds us of the incredible power of having a relationship with God, where impossibilities become opportunities for His greatness to shine. When we align ourselves with His promises, we can face what seems insurmountable knowing He sees possibilities where we only see barriers. God's power enables us to speak with boldness, declaring His will over our lives and trusting Him fully.

Picture this confidence as a child, surrounded by friends, confidently saying, "Dad will take care of the bill; he always does." This simple trust is the kind of faith we are called to have in God—a firm belief that He will provide and fulfill His promises.

Don't hesitate to declare the greatness of the God you serve. Speak boldly about what He can do, knowing He is always faithful. Trust Him in every circumstance, and don't hold back—He can do all things! Let your faith rise, and see His miracles unfold in your life.

Week 45 Monday

Above and Beyond

"The blood will be a sign for you on the houses where you are, and when I see the blood, I will pass over you. No destructive plague will touch you when I strike Egypt." (Exodus 12:13, NIV)

When the children of Israel were enslaved by Pharaoh, God sent plagues upon Egypt to secure their freedom. The final and most devastating plague was the death of all firstborn sons. To protect His people, God instructed the Israelites to place the blood of a lamb on their doorposts. When the death angel passed through, the blood marked their homes, sparing their families from harm. That night, while thousands of Egyptian firstborns lost their lives, the Israelites witnessed God's unfailing protection as He fulfilled His promise to safeguard those who obeyed Him.

This story is a powerful reminder of the lengths God will go to shield us from harm. Too often, we focus on what the enemy is doing instead of trusting in God's instructions for our lives. His guidance is our greatest defense. Just as the Israelites applied the lamb's blood to their doorposts, we can apply the blood of Jesus in prayer over our homes, anointing our spaces with oil and asking for His protection and presence.

God calls us to trust Him fully and let Him handle the battles we face. There is no enemy too strong for Him and no situation beyond His control. Follow His instructions, trust in His promises, and rest in His unfailing protection. He will go above and beyond to keep you and your loved ones safe. God's protection is steadfast—trust Him today!

Week 45 Tuesday

Nothing Can Stop

"He led them in safety, so that they were not afraid, but the sea overwhelmed their enemies." (Psalm 78:53, ESV)

Many of us have faced struggles in life that left us feeling hopeless, unable to see a way forward. In those moments, we may have battled sleepless nights, disrupted sleep patterns, changes in appetite, restlessness, difficulty concentrating, or even memory issues caused by relentless worry. Our anxiety may have soared with fears of the unknown, and our mood may have shifted, leaving us feeling weighed down by depression and unable to find the strength to face a new day.

Yet, through it all, God carried us. Even when we couldn't see it, He was working behind the scenes. He brought us through before, and He will continue to do so. The scripture reminds us that God led His people safely so they would not be afraid. He does the same for us—guiding us to a place of peace and safety where fear no longer holds power over us.

The scripture also says, "But the sea overwhelmed their enemies." God works on our behalf, often in ways we cannot fully comprehend. Just as Pharaoh and his army were no match for the force of the mighty rushing waters, no enemy can stand against the power of God.

Take heart and trust in His ability to bring you through life's challenges. His love and protection are unfailing, and His power is unmatched. God is always working for your good, even when the path seems unclear. Rest in Him and know that victory is in His hands!

Week 45 Wednesday

We Are Much Loved!

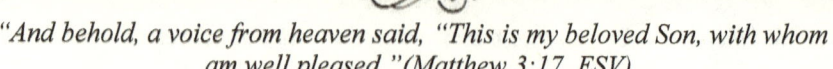

"And behold, a voice from heaven said, "This is my beloved Son, with whom I am well pleased." (Matthew 3:17, ESV)

Interestingly, before Jesus began His ministry, was tempted by the devil, died on the cross, and rose again, God spoke audibly from heaven, confirming that Jesus was His Son. This affirmation happened at the very beginning of His journey, showcasing the purpose and destiny already placed within Him. Like every young person, Jesus grew up, made choices, and experienced life, yet He stayed on track toward the destiny God designed for Him.

We are much the same, each of us navigating different stages of life, with a unique destiny ordained by God from the moment we were born until our time on earth ends. Regardless of where we stand today, we should be able to hear God's voice saying, "This is my beloved son/daughter, with whom I am well pleased." If we don't feel connected to His voice, it's worth reflecting on whether we're in the right place, doing what aligns with His plans for us.

Jesus positioned Himself to fulfill His destiny, and God affirmed it. Our lives are brief, like vapour, and we must be intentional not to waste them on distractions that pull us away from the purpose God has for us. Instead, we are called to listen for His voice, to seek His presence, and to align ourselves with His will.

Take a moment today to quiet your heart and listen for God's guidance. Wherever you are and in whatever you're doing, His voice is there to lead you toward your destiny. Trust Him to direct your path!

Week 45 Thursday

It's Coming After Us!

"Surely goodness and mercy shall follow me all the days of my life."
(Psalm 23:6, NKJV)

We live in a world where many things seem to follow us—beliefs, opinions, feelings, regrets, mistakes, bad habits, temptations, and even addictions. These are the shadows of life's challenges, constantly moving behind or coming after us, weighing us down. Yet, the scripture reminds us of a powerful truth: we are also followed by goodness and mercy. When David wrote, "Surely goodness and mercy shall follow me all the days of my life," he spoke with unwavering confidence, knowing that God's blessings were not only with him but ahead of him, turning his situation around.

David used the word "surely" intentionally, expressing his absolute assurance in God's promise. It wasn't a question of whether it was God's will—it was a declaration of certainty. This same confidence is available to us today. God's goodness and mercy are actively pursuing us, ready to overshadow the negativity and bring light into our lives.

It's time to let go of the things that weigh us down and allow God's goodness to win the race in our minds. His mercy is like bleach, cleansing our hearts and minds, leaving us renewed and refreshed. Let His love guide your path, filling your life with hope and purpose. Trust in His promises and walk forward confidently, knowing that His goodness and mercy will never fail to follow you, wherever life may lead. They are yours to embrace every day!

Week 45 Friday

God Laughs!!!

"He Who sits in the heavens laughs..." (Psalm 2:4, AMP)

Have you ever thought of God laughing? It's a heartwarming image, isn't it? Perhaps we inherited our sense of humor from Him. Laughter truly is a gift—it's good medicine for the soul. It has the power to bring people together, lifting spirits and changing emotions from sadness to joy. A good laugh can boost your mood, sweep away negative thoughts, and ease emotional pain. It shields you from stress and overwhelm, even brightening your outlook. Some even say it strengthens the immune system. Laughter inspires hope, helps us stay focused and grounded, and releases pent-up anger, leaving us lighter and freer.

God, seated on His throne, knows all the benefits of laughter and champions its power. He is not worried, upset, angry, or consumed with frustration. Instead, He laughs—because He sees things from an eternal perspective. God laughs knowing the enemy's days are numbered and that His ultimate victory is assured. He laughs because He sees the day when we will all be with Him, celebrating in joy and peace. He laughs because He knows each of our stories and how beautifully they will unfold. Most of all, He laughs with the confidence of a loving Father, trusting that we will overcome and triumph in every area of our lives.

Let His laughter remind you to embrace hope and joy. Know that just as He celebrates over you, His plans for your life are full of victory. Laugh with Him today, and let His joy carry you forward!

Week 46 Monday

God Chooses Our Steps!

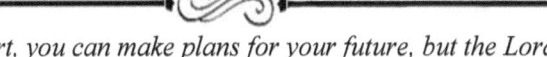

"Within your heart, you can make plans for your future, but the Lord chooses the steps you take to get there." (Proverbs 16:9, TPT)

Life often presents us with disappointments and challenges we never anticipated. These moments can leave us frustrated and discouraged, especially when we face situations we don't understand. In our minds, we carefully plan for the future, but when those plans fail, it can deepen our sense of discouragement.

Scripture reminds us that while we may create plans within our hearts, it is the Lord who ultimately determines our steps. Some of these steps may not align with what we envisioned, but God sees the entire picture of our lives—the beginning, the end, and everything in between. His perspective extends far beyond our own, and He knows the path that leads to success.

When we trust God and the steps He chooses for us, even if they seem unclear or unexpected, He works all things for our good. It's a gentle reminder not to act impulsively or try to force our way forward but to surrender our plans to Him. By aligning our desires with His will, we can trust that the outcomes will be far greater than anything we could accomplish on our own.

God's plans are always purposeful and full of hope. He lovingly guides us through the maze of life, leading us toward positive results and a fulfilling destiny. Take comfort in knowing that His way is always the best way. Trust in His guidance, align your plans with His today, and watch Him lead you to a place of peace and success.

Week 46 Tuesday
God Speaks Directly

"For those who are led by the Spirit of God are the children of God."
(Romans 8:14, NIV)

Sometimes, a name may cross our minds, a thought to give or help someone surfaces, or we feel a nudge to do good. These moments are not just random; they may be God speaking to us. At times, we sense something is wrong, often referred to as a "gut feeling." That, too, can be the Spirit of God prompting us to pay attention.

Perhaps you've been in a situation where someone's words deeply resonated with you, feeling as though they were speaking directly into your heart. It may very well have been God using them to reach you. I remember when someone asked me, "What do you really want for your life?" In that moment, it felt like God was speaking through them, bringing my inner thoughts to light and inspiring me to take action.

All too often, we overlook or dismiss these divine whispers and unintentionally miss out on opportunities to align ourselves with God's plan. The Spirit of God moves gently, and it's important to remain sensitive to His guidance. Instead of debating or doubting whether it's truly God speaking, we need to trust the promptings and let go of our desire to control everything.

Allow yourself to be led by the Spirit. Embrace those moments, trust in His guidance, and act in faith. When we surrender to His leading, we open the door to incredible opportunities and blessings in our lives. Listen, trust, and let God work through you!

Week 46 Wednesday

God's Timing Is Perfect!

"For still the vision awaits its appointed time...If it seems slow, wait for it; it will surely come; it will not delay." (Habakkuk 2:3, ESV)

Sometimes, we want something so deeply that it throws us off balance. We panic, worry, or feel like we're falling behind. Some may even wonder if God is listening, especially when the results we long for don't come as expected. From a young age, many of us are taught to rely on control—being told what to do and how to do it. It's no surprise that this mindset often carries into adulthood, making it hard to let go and trust.

However, control doesn't work with God. He is the only one we should allow to take full control of our lives. Unlike us, He sees the complete picture—tomorrow, the future, and every step we need to take to align with His plans. Even when we veer off track, He graciously realigns us, bringing us back to His purpose.

The scripture assures us that our vision has an appointed time. Though it may seem slow in coming, we are encouraged to wait for it, as it will surely come to pass. God's timing is never late; it is always perfect.

Let go of the urge to control every piece of your life. Trust in God to move the pieces into place at the right time. He knows exactly what you need and when you need it. Release your worries, rest in His plans, and watch as His purpose unfolds in ways greater than you could imagine. His timing is worth the wait!

Week 46 Thursday

God Got Your Back!

And Korah gathered all the congregation against them at the door of the tabernacle of meeting. Then the glory of the LORD appeared to all the congregation. "(Numbers 16:19, NKJV)

Korah, consumed by jealousy, led a rebellion against Moses's leadership, sowing seeds of discord and turning the nation against him. This act of division displeased God deeply, prompting Him to instruct Moses and Aaron to step away from the congregation so He could deal with the situation immediately. God's response reveals how much He disapproves of division and discontent among His people.

In our own lives, it's easy to get caught up in the negativity of others—whether it's the things they say against us or the seeds of discord they spread about others. Without realizing it, we can start believing their words, falling into the trap of bitterness, jealousy, and discontent. But God calls us to rise above these distractions. He challenges us not to participate in sowing discord and to remain focused on His purpose for our lives.

Some people cling to the past, holding onto ideas and actions that God has already disproved. What they see as normal may actually conflict with God's truth, creating confusion for others. We are reminded not to let these distractions pull us away from what God has planned for us

Trust God to handle the negativity and division around you. He is always in control, protecting and guiding you as you walk in His purpose. Keep your heart aligned with Him and let His strength carry you forward. God's support never wavers!

Week 46 Friday

Love and Faithfulness

"...those who plan what is good find love and faithfulness."
(Proverbs 14:22, NIV)

We all long for God's blessings and favor in our lives. But have we paused to ask ourselves—are we planning for what is good? Scripture teaches us that love is found when we plan for goodness. To truly experience God's presence and favor, we need to be intentional about living a life aligned with His will. As we create plans rooted in faith and purpose, God walks with us, opening doors we thought were closed, connecting us to the right people, and granting us unexpected favor.

When we allow God to guide our words and actions, His love flows through us, creating fruitfulness in every area of our lives. It's important to set intentional goals—short-term, long-term, and even miraculous ones—trusting Him to bring them to fruition in His perfect timing. As we surrender our plans to Him, we give God the opportunity to reveal Himself in extraordinary ways.

Jesus reminds us that we do not have because we do not ask. He encourages us to ask in His name and believe in the power of prayer. By aligning our plans with God's purpose, we position ourselves to see our destiny unfold. Love and faithfulness will follow when we trust Him completely and let Him take the lead.

Let God's promises guide your journey. Seek His presence, align your steps with His, and watch how His favor and blessings transform your life. Love and faithfulness will surely follow you all the days of your life!

Week 47 Monday

We Are Not A Label!

"I praise you because I am fearfully and wonderfully made; your works are wonderful, I know that full well." (Psalm 139:14, NIV)

In today's world, people are free to express their opinions, share their perceptions, and voice their feelings openly. Unfortunately, this freedom sometimes leads to the projection of negative labels onto others. We've all experienced moments when someone has said what they think we can't do or who they think we are—emotional bullying that can sting deeply. Over time, we may begin to believe these words, labeling ourselves as mistakes, disappointments, unworthy, or simply not good enough.

But scripture reminds us of a greater truth: we are fearfully and wonderfully made by God. He created us with care and intention, perfect in His design. Though sin may have corrupted parts of our body, soul, and spirit, God's handiwork remains beautiful and purposeful. When we look at the works of the Lord, we can see the beauty of who we were created to be—unique, loved, and valued in His sight.

Our spirit, crafted by God, reflects His image and uniqueness. By living in the Spirit, we connect with the depth of who we are in Christ. We find strength and confidence in knowing that His love defines us—not the opinions or perceptions of others.

Take time to appreciate the beauty of who you are in Christ. Let His truth drown out the negativity and embrace the identity He has given you. You are wonderfully made, and His Spirit within you is a reminder of your worth and purpose. Live boldly in this truth today!

Week 47 Tuesday

Captures God's Attention!

"When the Lord saw the grieving mother, his heart broke for her. With great tenderness, he said to her, "Please don't cry." (Luke 7:13, TPT)

This story recounts a heart-wrenching moment—a funeral procession for a widow's son. She had already endured the loss of her husband, and now her only son was gone. As a mother, her grief and emotional pain were unimaginable, leaving her heartbroken and wounded. But amid her sorrow, Jesus saw her pain. Her anguish captured His attention and moved Him with compassion.

Many of us have felt emotionally wounded, overwhelmed by loneliness or grief. Just as Jesus saw the widow's pain, He sees yours. He understands the depth of your struggles and feels your hurt. His compassion is unchanging, and He will make a way through whatever overwhelms you.

When Jesus told the widow not to weep, He touched the coffin and brought her son back to life, turning her sorrow into joy. He wants to do the same for us. Jesus can transform our weeping into great joy and bring healing to the brokenness within us. He recognizes the issues that cause emotional pain, and when we invite Him into our lives, He intervenes with peace that surpasses all understanding.

Our sadness and brokenness never go unnoticed by God. His love and compassion are constant, and He is always ready to bring healing. Trust Him with your pain and allow Him to work in your life. Jesus is the same yesterday, today, and forever. Give your burdens over to Him, and let His peace and joy renew your heart. He is always near.

Week 47 Wednesday
There Is Strength In Jesus!

"Though you have not seen him, you love him; and even though you do not see him now, you believe in him and are filled with an inexpressible and glorious joy." (1 Peter 1:8, NIV)

Life's challenges and overwhelming demands can leave us feeling drained, weighed down by anxiety, depression, and exhaustion. But this was never God's intention for us. He wants us to live with joy, peace, and hope. To experience this, we must consciously choose to shift our perspective—stimulating our hearts and minds to embrace positivity and relying on God for the daily strength we need to move forward.

Scripture reminds us, "Though we have not seen Him, we love Him; even though we do not see Him now, we believe in Him and are filled with inexpressible and glorious joy." This truth encourages us to focus on the depth of God's love and the joy that comes from believing in His presence and promises.

Take time to reflect on all that Jesus has done for you—the miracles, blessings, and moments when His hand moved powerfully in your life. Let these memories reignite your faith, making it stronger with each passing day. As we dwell on God's love and trust in His ability to do the impossible, our burdens begin to feel lighter, and hope fills our hearts.

Let's focus our thoughts today on who God is and what He can do. Trust Him completely, knowing He is greater than any circumstance. His strength and joy are always available to sustain you. Believe in His promises and embrace the glorious joy that flows from His unfailing love!

Week 47 Thursday

Like Cold Water

"Two are better than one, because they have a good return for their labor: If either of them falls down, one can help the other up."
(Ecclesiastes 4:9–10, NIV)

In the busyness of life, we often face unforeseen challenges and obstacles that test our strength and resolve. During these times, we may seek prayers and encouragement from others, but it's important to be mindful of who we allow to speak into our lives. Not everyone who surrounds us brings life and hope—some may struggle with insecurities, jealousy, or envy, speaking negativity and discouragement instead. These voices, like cold water, can dampen our faith and stir up doubt and fear.

Guarding our hearts from such influences is essential, as doubt can hinder the breakthroughs we're striving for. Instead, surround yourself with those who uplift you, who align their faith with yours, and who stand boldly for the impossible alongside you. Scripture reminds us, "Two are better than one, because they have a good return for their labor: If either of them falls down, one can help the other up." The power of agreement unleashes strength and shatters limitations.

Choose to walk with those who speak life into your circumstances, who build your faith and encourage your heart. Together, you can face obstacles and stand firm in God's promises. Be intentional about whom you allow into your inner circle, inviting those who will nurture your faith and stand steadfast in prayer and belief.

When you stand united with others in faith, strength is multiplied, and breakthroughs become possible. Trust in the power of agreement and let God's love and support lead the way forward!

Week 47 Friday

God Is Never Afraid!

"You've supercharged my life so that I soar again like a flying eagle in the sky!" (Psalm 103:5, TPT)

David wrote with deep insight into his experiences with God, reflecting on His faithfulness and power. Imagine the first time David stood before Goliath—a giant whose size and strength had terrified an entire army. What thoughts ran through his mind? Did he compare this challenge to the obstacles he had faced as a shepherd boy, protecting his sheep? Did he question his own abilities, thinking he was too young, inexperienced, or untrained to fight such a battle?

Instead of focusing on his limitations, David fixed his eyes on the limitless power of God. He had unwavering confidence that the same God who had delivered him from the lion and the bear would also deliver him from the giant. David's faith wasn't rooted in his own strength but in God's proven ability to overcome the impossible.

This story reminds us to trust in God's power when faced with life's challenges. We don't need to second-guess ourselves or give in to fear when obstacles arise. The experiences we've had with God—however limited—are enough to carry us through. Like David, we must stand with bold confidence, knowing that no challenge is too big for God.

God isn't afraid or overwhelmed by our requests. He doesn't need time to regain His strength or figure things out. He is ever-present, ready to supercharge us with courage, strength, and faith to face every obstacle. Trust Him completely, and watch Him work in your life!

Week 48 Monday

God Will Align Your Life!

"You've supercharged my life so that I soar again like a flying eagle in the sky!" (Psalm 103:5, TPT)

David was anointed by Samuel to be the next king of Israel. However, instead of stepping straight into the palace, he returned to tending his father's sheep. Faithful in what he knew to do best, David approached his work with joy and diligence. In time, word of his talent likely began to spread, and God used this to align his path with King Saul.

As king, Saul faced immense stress—perhaps even anxiety or depression. He needed someone to play soothing music to bring him peace. This is when David, the young shepherd boy who excelled in playing the harp, was called upon. God orchestrated the opportunity and opened the doors for David to step into the king's presence, using his gifts to make a difference.

This story reminds us to remain faithful wherever God has placed us. By focusing on our strengths and working with joy, we prepare ourselves for the opportunities God will bring. He will align our lives with the right people at the right time, opening doors we could never imagine and positioning us for our destiny.

It's important not to be distracted by what others have or where they are in life. God has a unique plan for each of us. Just as King Saul sought out David, someone will seek you for the gifts and talents God has placed within you. Keep nurturing those gifts, gaining experience, and trusting His perfect timing. Your faithfulness will lead to extraordinary opportunities!

Week 48 Tuesday
We Are Not Alone!

"The Lord himself goes before you and will be with you; he will never leave you nor forsake you. Do not be afraid; do not be discouraged."
(Deuteronomy 31:8, NIV)

This scripture reminds me of a precious moment with our daughter Kristan when she was about three years old. She came to us one day and said, "Jesus walked into my room and kissed me, saying He will come back." I was away that day, and she waited the entire day for me to return so she could share this experience. At the time, we were missionaries in Croatia, struggling through the challenges of war. I asked her, "How do you know it was Jesus?" With unwavering certainty, she replied, "He was dressed in white, and I just know."

This tender memory is a reminder of God's promises to us. He assures us that He will never leave us or forsake us, no matter the battles, trials, or challenges we face. Even when we can't see what He is doing, God is always at work, orchestrating His best for us.

The scripture tells us that the Lord Himself will go before us and be with us, wherever we are in life. We are encouraged not to be afraid or discouraged, knowing His presence is constant and His love unwavering.

It's easy to focus on life's challenges and let fear cloud our vision. But let's fix our eyes on God and His faithfulness. Don't lose sight of His hand in your life. Trust that He is always by your side, working on your behalf, and guiding you through every obstacle with love and purpose.

Week 48 Wednesday

Unshakable and Assured!

"I've told you all this so that trusting me, you will be unshakable and assured, deeply at peace. In this godless world, you will continue to experience difficulties. But take heart! I've conquered the world." (John 16:33, MSG)

Jesus, in His timeless wisdom, spoke to His disciples about the reality of living in a world that often feels distant from God. This truth remains unchanged and, in many ways, has grown more challenging. Life today is filled with demands that pull at our attention—pressures from work, relationships, societal expectations, and countless disruptions. We are constantly faced with questions about our beliefs, morals, and faith, making it easy to feel overwhelmed.

Yet, amidst this chaos, there is hope. When we place our trust in Jesus, we can stand firm, unshakable in the storms of life. His peace becomes our refuge, and we can rest assured that we are held in His loving care. Just as Jesus overcame the trials of this world, we too can overcome, as long as we invite Him to journey with us. His plan and purpose for our lives remain steadfast, unaltered by the challenges we face. His love and His promises are constant, offering us guidance and strength.

Today, take a step of faith and place your trust in the Lord. Do not rely solely on your own understanding, for it can lead to uncertainty. Instead, in every moment and every decision, acknowledge Him, and He will faithfully guide your path. Jesus's peace and love are yours to embrace, bringing calm and assurance to even the most turbulent times. Trust in Him, and you will find the strength to rise above.

Week 48 Thursday
Stick With God's Plan!

"Please pay no attention, my lord, to that wicked man Nabal. He is just like his name— his name means Fool, and folly goes with him."
(1 Samuel 25:25, NIV)

Nabal was a wealthy man known for being difficult and harsh, often impossible to get along with. His offensive behavior and mean-spirited actions stirred up deep anger in David, prompting him to command four hundred of his men to exact revenge by killing Nabal and his men. Caught in his emotions, David was overwhelmed by feelings of hurt and outrage, which clouded his judgment and nearly led him down a dangerous path of shedding innocent blood. Such a choice could have drastically altered and hindered the destiny God had planned for him.

In this moment, Abigail, Nabal's wife, played a pivotal role. With wisdom and grace, she approached David and helped him recognize the foolishness of her husband's behavior. She reminded David of the greater purpose God had set before him, steering him away from actions he might regret.

Much like David, we often encounter people who are difficult to connect with—those whose behavior feels like "oil and vinegar," always in conflict. Some individuals are rude, offensive, or self-absorbed, and their actions can trigger strong emotions within us.

In times like these, we need the "Abigails" in our lives—wise and discerning individuals who remind us of our destiny and help us see the futility in reacting to the negativity of others. Stay rooted in God's plan and purpose, and let Him guide you through life's challenges without distraction.

Week 48 Friday

Allow The Lion To Rise Up!

"The righteous are as bold as a lion." (Proverbs 28:1, NIV)

Lions are symbols of courage, strength, and unity, living as part of a pride and carrying themselves with unmatched confidence. Despite being "just a cat," they are rightfully regarded as the king of the animal kingdom. This title is not based on being the strongest, tallest, or wisest—there are other animals that surpass them in these traits. Yet, lions embody boldness, believing deeply in their own ability to remain undefeated.

Similarly, we often find ourselves questioning what we can and cannot achieve, doubting our worth or potential. But we must not measure our future by the limitations or challenges we face today. Each of us has something unique and valuable to offer, and we should never let insecurities hold us back from embracing our inner strength.

Scripture calls us to be as bold as lions, reminding us to wear our crown of courage, no matter the circumstances. Even if others around us may appear stronger, wiser, or more experienced, it is our faith and boldness that empower us to rise above fear and self-doubt.

Let this inspire you to step out of the grip of anxiety and fear, and allow the lion within you to roar with confidence and purpose. Boldness is not about the absence of challenges—it's about the willingness to face them head-on, trusting that you are equipped with the strength to overcome. Embrace your potential, walk in faith, and let your lion-hearted spirit shine.

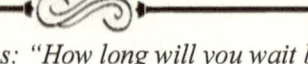

Take Possession!

"So Joshua said to the Israelites: "How long will you wait before you begin to take possession of the land that the LORD, the God of your ancestors, has given you?" (Joshua 18:3, NIV)

God entrusted the Israelites with the land of Canaan, the Promised Land, as a gift to them. However, they needed to step forward and take possession of it, learning to claim and embrace what God had already provided. Despite this incredible promise, the Israelites found themselves paralyzed by fear of the giants in the land. Their hesitation reflected a struggle to fully trust in God's provision and the strength He had already given them. Joshua had to challenge them with a powerful question: "How long will you wait before you begin to take possession of the land that the LORD, the God of your ancestors, has given you?"

Similarly, many of us find ourselves waiting, hesitant to claim the blessings God has already set before us. Whether it's your job, marriage, finances, relationships, healing, or other gifts, the Lord's provision is yours. What He has given you, no one can take away. Yet, fears, anxieties, or the "giants" in our lives often stand in the way, causing hesitation and doubt.

Today, let this be an encouragement to place your confidence in the Lord. Do not let fear or uncertainty hold you back. Rise above the challenges, trusting in God's plan and His strength to equip you for every step. His blessings are already yours—step out in faith, take possession of them, and walk boldly in His promises. The giants may seem overwhelming, but God is far greater, and His purpose for you is steadfast. Let your trust in Him lead the way.

Week 49 Tuesday

Courteous, Kind & Pleasant!

"Yet the LORD longs to be gracious to you; therefore he will rise to show you compassion.... Blessed are all who wait for him!" (Isaiah 30:18, NIV)

This scripture serves as a beautiful reminder of God's unwavering grace and kindness toward us. It reveals His nature as courteous, kind, and pleasant, always extending divine mercy to our failures, weaknesses, and mistakes. Yet, many of us struggle to move beyond our past, allowing it to cheat us of the goodness and blessings that God intends for our lives and families.

When we remain stuck in what has been, we risk missing out on the full potential God has placed within us. Holding onto fears and doubts can suppress our faith, giving the enemy a foothold to keep us from embracing His favor. Even our dreams can begin to fade as we lose hope and believe that obstacles are too great to overcome.

However, the scripture reminds us of a profound truth: "Yet the LORD longs to be gracious to you." God eagerly desires to extend His kindness and compassion to us. His love is not fleeting or conditional—it rises above our struggles and envelops us in His care. This compassion is a deep and abiding sympathy for our suffering, coupled with the desire to bring us healing and peace.

The verse concludes with encouragement: "Blessed are all who wait for him!" Waiting on the Lord is an act of faith, trusting in His timing and His perfect plans for us. As we wait, we can rest in the assurance that His grace and favor will carry us through life's challenges, leading us toward His promises. Let us lean on His kindness and embrace the blessings He longs to pour into our lives.

Week 49 Wednesday

The Power of Honour!

"Give everyone what you owe them...if honour, then honour."
(Romans 13:7, NIV)

Honour holds great significance in the eyes of God, as emphasized throughout the Bible. In Exodus, we are reminded to honour our parents with the promise of a long life as a reward. Proverbs teaches us that prosperity and honour will follow those who pursue righteousness, reaffirming the blessings that come from a life lived in alignment with God's will.

There is a distinct difference between loyalty and honour. David honoured King Saul and preserved his life, while Jonathan was loyal and tragically met his end. Honour involves showing genuine recognition and respect through our words, actions, and behaviors.

When we honor others, especially in the spaces God has guided us to, He promises to bless and reward us. This requires us to rise above our emotions and feelings, focusing instead on embracing the relationships and responsibilities God has entrusted to us.

Living a righteous life that seeks to please God and align with His expectations opens the door to His favor and blessings, just as His Word assures us. Honour is not about empty words but about actions that reflect our faith, humility, and obedience to Him.

Take the step to show honour to those God has placed in your life. Let your actions speak louder than words, and trust that God will fulfill His promises as you walk in righteousness and respect. Honour brings us closer to God's heart and invites His blessings into our lives.

Week 49 Thursday

Expect The Unexpected

"But Simon answered and said to Him, "Master, we have toiled all night and caught nothing; nevertheless, at Your word, I will let down the net."
(Luke 5:5, NKJV)

This is a story of faith and trust, where Jesus spoke to Peter, a seasoned fisherman, who had worked tirelessly all night, casting his net into deep waters without catching a single fish. As morning arrived, Jesus instructed Peter to try again and throw his net into the water. For Peter, who was deeply familiar with fishing and knew how difficult it was to catch fish during daylight hours, this request didn't align with his logical understanding.

Despite his doubts, Peter chose to obey Jesus's words, even though it didn't make sense to him. To his astonishment, his nets became so full of fish that they began to break under the weight. This miraculous moment revealed the power of trusting God's word over human reasoning and logic.

In our lives, there are moments when we let our logical minds take control, allowing doubt to cloud our faith. The impossible becomes possible when we believe in the promises of the Lord.

No matter the challenges you're facing or the struggles that weigh you down, choose faith over doubt. Like Peter, say, "Nevertheless, at Your word," and allow God to work miracles in your life. Trust in Him, and expect the unexpected, knowing that His plans for you are greater than anything you could imagine. Let faith guide you beyond the limits of logic and into the fullness of God's blessings.

Week 49 Friday

The Encouraging Heart

"Encourage the hearts of your fellow believers and support one another, just as you have already been doing." (1 Thessalonians 5:11, TPT)

In today's fast-paced world, the demands on our time and energy feel endless. It often seems like 24 hours in a day are simply not enough to take a moment for ourselves. Time with family is often limited, overshadowed by work and other pressing responsibilities. Just like anything that's used continuously, we can become worn out. Many of us find ourselves burnt out, unable to pause and enjoy life—whether it's taking up a hobby, savoring a coffee with a friend, or spending quality time with loved ones.

Even as we strive to balance responsibilities, we may face criticism for trying to prioritize our well-being. Yet, the scripture reminds us to "encourage the hearts of your fellow believers and support one another, just as you have already been doing." Offering moral support to one another is a priceless gift that helps ease the weight of life's demands. It bridges the gap created by our busy schedules and restores a sense of connection.

Take a moment today to reach out to someone—whether it's a friend or a family member. A simple greeting, a quick "hi," can be like a spark of energy, brightening someone's day. The kindness you sow will always come back to you in beautiful ways. Let us remember to uplift one another, supporting each other in ways that refresh our spirits and deepen our bonds. Together, we can overcome the challenges of our demanding lives and rediscover joy in the moments we share.

Week 50 Monday

His Timing Is Perfect

"For since the world began, no ear has heard, and no eye has seen a God like you, who works for those who wait for him!" (Isaiah 64:4, NLT)

What a beautiful reminder that God is always at work for those who wait on Him. Life often brings moments that leave us questioning why certain things happen. Negative encounters can weigh heavily on our hearts, leaving behind bitterness and strife. Yet, we are called to let go of those burdens and trust that God will work all things together for our good. Though we may not understand the "why" in the present, one day His purpose will become clear.

It is essential to remain steadfast in keeping God's presence over our lives and our loved ones. His protection surrounds us, even in the midst of challenges. Keep trusting Him, no matter how difficult the road may seem. Learning to walk away from pain and disappointment and surrendering them to God allows His promises to shine through. He will bring beauty from the ashes and joy to replace our mourning.

Continue to do the right thing, and never stop lifting your heart in praise. Complaining will not change your circumstances, but God can. He is always working behind the scenes, orchestrating solutions and blessings at the perfect time. His timing is never early or late—it is always right.

Be encouraged today. Hold on to hope and trust that the solution you seek is closer than it seems. God's plans are never delayed. He is the beginning and the ending, and His faithfulness will carry you through to fulfillment and peace. Keep believing!

Week 50 Tuesday

He Will Restore It

"For I will restore health to you and heal you of your wounds," says the LORD." (Jeremiah 30:17, NKJV)

Life often presents us with setbacks, disappointments, and unexpected challenges—whether through financial struggles, illnesses, relationship difficulties, employment issues, or moments we simply didn't see coming. It's natural to feel weighed down by these hardships, and in those moments, some of us may find ourselves blaming others, blaming God, or even blaming ourselves. Yet, it's important to remember that when we are walking on the right path, the enemy may try to throw obstacles in our way, tempting us and leading to further difficulties.

God never promised that life would be without struggles, but He did promise that He would bring restoration. For those of us who feel that life's stressors have taken a toll on our mental health and physical well-being, God assures us of His healing and correction. As He declares, "I will restore your health and heal you of your wounds." These words are a promise of renewal, hope, and strength.

Whatever challenges you may be facing, bring them before the Lord and leave them at His feet. Trust that God does not judge you or turn away when you falter or make mistakes. Instead, He welcomes you with open arms, ready to embrace and restore you. His love is unwavering, and His grace is abundant. Hold onto His promises and keep your faith strong, knowing that God works all things together for your good. Restoration is not just possible—it is promised. Let Him heal and renew your spirit!

Week 50 Wednesday

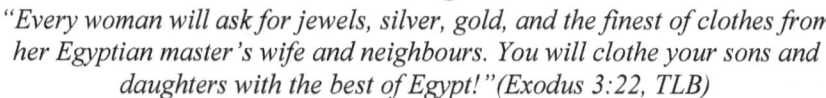
Going To A Wedding

"Every woman will ask for jewels, silver, gold, and the finest of clothes from her Egyptian master's wife and neighbours. You will clothe your sons and daughters with the best of Egypt!" (Exodus 3:22, TLB)

When God delivered the Israelites after 430 years of slavery in Egypt, He didn't just free them—He restored their dignity. He directed their oppressors to give them gold, silver, and fine clothing as a form of repayment for the generations of suffering they endured. But God's plan was deeper than material compensation. After years of enslavement, the Israelites had developed a victim mindset, one that weighed heavily on how they saw themselves. God wanted to transform that perception. He wanted them to stop seeing themselves as poor, broken, or defeated, and instead view themselves the way He did—valued, cherished, and worthy of the best.

To solidify this new perspective, God instructed the parents to dress their sons and daughters in jewelry and fine clothing. This symbolic act allowed them to walk out of Egypt not as victims, but as royalty. Even though their destination was the desert, they were dressed as though they were heading to a grand celebration, reminding them that their identity was rooted in God's promises, not their circumstances.

In life, we can find ourselves feeling beaten down or defeated, seeing ourselves through a lens of struggle rather than triumph. But God calls us to rise above that. Wherever you're headed, walk into it with confidence, like royalty. Even if the journey feels like a desert, carry yourself as though you're stepping into a celebration. Trust that God's promises are greater than your challenges and that His plans for you are filled with honor, restoration, and hope. Dress for the victory He has already prepared!

Week 50 Thursday

Broken Teeth

The lions may roar and growl, yet the teeth of the great lions are broken."
(Job 4:10, NIV)

The lion, often seen as the king of the animal kingdom, is a fascinating creature. Despite being smaller, less intelligent, and less powerful than other animals, the lion commands respect. Known for their territorial nature and confident stride, lions, though just cats, evoke fear with their mighty roars, intimidating those who dare cross their path.

Similarly, the challenges and fears we face can act like roaring lions in our lives, attempting to intimidate and paralyze us. These "roars" of negativity and doubt may fill us with anxiety, causing us to question our ability to move forward. When the path ahead seems dangerous, or fear looms large, it's easy to lose hope. But we are reminded in the book of Job that "the lions" may roar and growl, yet their teeth have been broken. Their threats are hollow.

In 1 Peter 5:8, it says, "Be sober-minded; be watchful. Your adversary the devil prowls around like a roaring lion, seeking someone to devour." This scripture encourages us not to allow fear or negativity to stop us from pursuing the destiny God has for us. The roars of the enemy may be loud, but they are powerless in the presence of God's promises.

Stand strong in faith and resist the roar of doubt. Remember, the lion's teeth have been broken—its power is an illusion. Trust in God's guidance, and press forward with courage toward the purpose He has set before you. The victory is yours!

Week 50 Friday

Carry That Weight?

"Cast your burden on the Lord [releasing the weight of it], and He will sustain you." (Psalm 55:22, AMPC)

As a young boy, growing up without running water or electricity, life was full of responsibilities that taught me the meaning of carrying burdens. One of my daily tasks was to gather dry wood from the forest for cooking. I can still vividly recall walking for over an hour, with a heavy bundle balanced on my head, feeling the weight of every step. Another task was fetching clean drinking water from a tap three kilometers away. Carrying those heavy containers home would strain my arms and leave me exhausted.

Reflecting on those memories, I see how they mirror the emotional and spiritual weights many of us carry today—fears, anxieties, regrets, mistakes, and the pain caused by others. These invisible burdens can be just as exhausting, draining our strength and stealing our peace.

But there is hope. Jesus invites us to bring these weights to Him, assuring us that He will sustain us. He offers strength and support for every aspect of our being—physically, mentally, emotionally, and spiritually. His promise is not just to help us carry the load, but to lighten it entirely.

Don't let the pressures of life weigh you down or keep you from the abundant life God has planned for you. Whatever burdens you are carrying, give them to the Lord. Trust in His sustaining power, and let Him renew your strength and restore your peace. In His hands, your burdens will become light, and you will find rest for your soul.

Week 51 Monday

Your Are Enough

"The devil led him to Jerusalem and had him stand on the temple's highest point. "If you are the Son of God," he said, "throw yourself down from here." (Luke 4:9, NIV)

The devil sought to use Jesus as a spectacle, aiming to display His power to impress the people at the temple. His plan was rooted in manipulation, tempting Jesus to act with motives of pride and self-glorification. However, Jesus remained steadfast in His purpose, refusing to misuse His divine power for selfish reasons. He did not seek to bring attention to Himself or prove His worth through grand displays, even though He had the ability to walk on water or summon thousands of angels. Jesus understood that His ministry was not about impressing others or proving His identity—it was about fulfilling God's will with humility and integrity.

This example speaks powerfully to our own lives. We do not need to prove our worth or value to anyone. The motives behind our actions should be grounded in goodness and purpose, not in seeking approval or validation. Impressing others is never the goal; instead, we can trust in God to show up with His divine power at the right time. His intervention is always rooted in love, not to prove a point or bring glory to us, but to fulfill His plans.

Today, let this truth remind you that your self-worth is not dependent on the opinions or validations of others. God sees your heart, your intentions, and your unique value. That is all that truly matters. Rest in His assurance, knowing that your worth comes from Him alone, and His love is unwavering. You are enough!

Week 51 Tuesday

Called To Prosper!

"Be strong and very courageous, ...; do not turn from it to the right hand or to the left, that you may prosper wherever you go." (Joshua 1:7, NKJV)

We are reminded to be strong and courageous, keeping our focus on the destiny God has set before us. To prosper in life means more than just succeeding—it means thriving and living vibrantly. God's desire is for us to prosper, but this requires staying on the path He has laid out for us. While obstacles and challenges will inevitably arise, we can trust that God always has a plan to guide us through. Though the enemy may attempt to divert us from His purpose, God is faithful to steer us back on track when we stumble.

The key to living in God's abundance is following His instructions. When we align our lives with His word, we open the door to true prosperity. As 3 John 2 says, "Beloved, I pray that you may prosper in all things and be in health, just as your soul prospers." Our spiritual health, rooted in strength and courage, is essential for keeping us anchored in our purpose and destiny.

Take a moment to reflect: What are the most important things in your life right now, and how are you prioritizing them? Let this be your guidepost as you navigate life's journey. Remember, God's plan for you is always for good, and He equips you with everything you need to succeed. Stay bold, stay focused, and trust that His blessings will flow as you walk in faith and courage. Keep your heart on the pathway He has assigned to you, and you will thrive.

Week 51 Wednesday

Appreciate Yourself!

"But He answered him not one word so that the governor marvelled greatly."
(Matthew 27:14, NKJV)

Throughout His ministry, Jesus faced relentless criticism, hurtful words, false accusations, and disapproval from many people. Despite having the power to summon ten thousand angels to defend Himself or prove His worth, Jesus chose instead to remain focused on His purpose and goals. Even when brought to trial before Pilate and accused unjustly, He did not defend Himself or utter a single word in response. His silence reflected profound strength and unwavering confidence in His identity and mission.

This teaches us an important lesson: when we are secure in who we are, we don't need to justify ourselves to others. We don't need to prove our knowledge, our worth, or our value. Insecurities and self-doubt can often lead us to feel the need to answer every criticism, defend every action, or resolve every problem. Yet, there is wisdom in sometimes choosing silence—refusing to be drawn into negativity or the traps others might set.

While we cannot stop people from being critical or negative, we can choose how we respond. By appreciating ourselves and staying committed to our goals and purpose, we prevent external voices from distracting or discouraging us. Just as Jesus showed, strength is not always in defending oneself—it can often be found in quiet determination to stay true to the path God has placed before us. Keep your focus, and trust that your worth comes from God, not from the approval of others. Walk confidently in His purpose for you!

Week 51 Thursday

Take In The Sun!

"For the Lord God is a sun and shield; the Lord bestows favour and honour; no good thing does he withhold from those whose walk is blameless."
(Psalm 84:11, NIV)

It's fascinating how many of us love soaking in the sun's warmth, especially by the water. Sunlight feels comforting and is vital for our health and well-being. It provides vitamin D, strengthens our bones, lowers blood pressure, prevents illnesses, and supports mental health. Just as sunlight nurtures our bodies, God nurtures our souls. He is our eternal sun, offering His warmth and light without ever causing harm. As our shield, He protects us from the enemy and surrounds us with His favor and honor.

Scripture reminds us, "No good thing does he withhold from those whose walk is blameless." This isn't a call to perfection—it's about the name God has given us when we come to Him. Through His grace, He calls us blameless, inviting us to walk in the identity He has gifted us. Even when we stumble or make mistakes, He is faithful to forgive and cleanse us, as promised in 1 John 1:9: "If we confess our sins, He is faithful and just to forgive us our sins and to cleanse us from all unrighteousness."

Let's lean into God's radiant presence, embracing Him as both our sun and shield. Tap into His unending favor, and trust in the blessings He longs to pour into our lives. His goodness is abundant and available to us all. Walk in His light today, and let His love and protection guide your every step!

Week 51 Friday

He Is There!

"Where can I flee from your presence? If I go up to the heavens, you are there; if I make my bed in the depths, you are there." (Psalm 139:7–8, NIV)

There are moments in life when we may feel distant from God or believe we've reached a place where His presence cannot find us. One police officer once shared his story during the war in Croatia, saying he thought his actions had placed him beyond God's reach. Yet, God touched his heart and freed him from the lies the enemy had planted in his mind. This is a powerful reminder that no matter our mistakes, flaws, or regrets, we are never beyond God's reach.

God does not hold our weaknesses or past choices against us. His love for us is unwavering and far too great to leave us in a place of hopelessness. He is right there with you, ready to forgive, not condemn. His mercy renews every morning, bringing fresh grace to our lives. Only God can release your mind from the grip of guilt and shame, lifting you up and placing you back on the path to your destiny.

The plans He has for your life remain intact, and He will faithfully complete the good work He started in you. He will reveal the greatness within you, allowing His goodness to pursue and overwhelm you. Even when you feel you've missed out or veered off course, God can propel you forward into the future He has prepared for you. Trust in His faithfulness and let His love guide you into a life of hope and restoration. God is always with you, and His promises endure forever.

Week 52 Monday

Born To Win!

"And let us run with endurance the race God has set before us."
(Hebrews 12:1, NLT)

God has set each of us on a unique path—a race where we are destined to reach the finish line. This race is not about proving your worth to others or defeating them; it is about recognizing the victory God has already placed within you. He made you a winner, a champion, and a hero, crafted in His image and likeness. God Himself has never been defeated. He never gives up, He never quits, and He calls us to follow His example with unwavering perseverance.

We must release the pressure of trying to impress others or seeking their approval. Carrying the weight of proving ourselves can be exhausting, and it pulls us away from the freedom God intends for us. Comparing ourselves to others only builds insecurities and feeds thoughts of inadequacy, creating low self-esteem that can cripple our confidence. These doubts are not from God, who sees us as fully capable and prepared for the race He has placed before us.

No matter the obstacles you face, God believes in your ability to overcome. He has equipped you with the resilience to rise above challenges and keep moving forward. You don't need to measure yourself against others or let self-doubt hold you back. Trust in God's plan and know that you were born to win. Step into your race with courage, confidence, and faith, knowing that your victory is assured. Keep your eyes on the finish line—God is with you every step of the way!

Week 52 Tuesday

It Started and Ended

"He told them, "My soul is crushed with grief to the point of death. Stay here and keep watch with me." (Matthew 26:38, NLT)

It began in the garden of Eden, where humanity first disobeyed God, and it was brought to completion in the garden of Gethsemane, where Jesus redeemed what was broken. In Eden, God created man to worship Him and build a relationship—a sacred meeting place with their Creator. Yet, disobedience entered the story, altering the purpose of the garden. In Gethsemane, Jesus bore the weight of that disobedience, paying the ultimate price on our behalf. Despite asking His disciples to keep watch, they fell asleep, weary and frustrated, leaving Him to face the burden alone.

Gethsemane has now become our new Eden—a place of restoration through Christ. It is a reminder to stay vigilant, to pray for our families, friends, and the world, and to bring our needs before God. Just as Jesus approached the Father with His deepest burdens in the garden, we are invited to do the same, especially during times of disappointment and struggle.

Though exhaustion and frustration may weigh us down, God has renewed our strength so we can keep watch and pray. He has given us the ability to stand firm and seek Him with boldness. Gethsemane represents the place where restoration and hope are born, and it calls us to connect with God's promises.

Watch and pray—seek Him wholeheartedly, trusting that He will bring healing and transformation. What began in the garden has been redeemed in the garden, through the sacrifice of Jesus. Let us honor Him by keeping our hearts devoted to prayer and faith.

Week 52 Wednesday

Call It Blessing!

"On the fourth day they gathered in the Valley of Blessing, which got its name that day because the people praised and thanked the LORD there."
(2 Chronicles 20:26, NLT)

The valley earned its name, "The Valley of Blessing," after King Jehoshaphat demonstrated unwavering obedience to the Lord's guidance. He was instructed to lead his army toward three mighty forces—the Moabites, the Ammonites, and the Meunites—who had joined together to wage war against Judah and the people of Jerusalem. Despite the overwhelming odds, Jehoshaphat trusted God and prepared his army as instructed. As they marched forward, they began to sing and praise, lifting their voices in worship. Miraculously, the Bible tells us that the Lord set ambushes against the invading armies, causing confusion among them. In the chaos, the enemies turned against one another and fought among themselves until they were defeated.

This valley could have been named after fear, struggle, or defeat, but instead, it was given a name that speaks to God's power and goodness—the Valley of Blessing. It stands as a reminder of how battles in life can transform into testimonies of victory when we trust in God.

In our own lives, we must learn to see challenges not as defeats, but as opportunities for blessing and triumph. By registering positive affirmations in our minds and focusing on God's faithfulness, we can shift our perspective. Celebrate your victories, no matter how small, and give praise to the Lord for His goodness and provision. The Lord's blessings are always at work, even in the midst of our battles. Keep your heart anchored in gratitude and trust Him to bring victory!

Week 52 Thursday

It Took All Night!

"Then Moses stretched out his hand over the sea, and all that night the LORD drove the sea back with a strong east wind and turned it into dry land. The waters were divided..." (Exodus 14:21, NIV)

The story of the Israelites' exodus from Egypt is powerful, especially when we know how it ends. But imagine the fear and chaos they must have felt as they fled. With Pharaoh and his army pursuing them, the air was filled with panic—the yelling, crying, and unpredictability of families desperately running with their children. Doubts and fears must have overwhelmed their hearts. Then, to add to their stress, they saw a storm ahead.

When God parted the waters of the Red Sea, the scripture says, "and all that night the LORD drove the sea back with a strong east wind and turned it into dry land." The process took all night, requiring patience and faith as they faced the storm. It's easy to think they may have viewed the storm as yet another obstacle, perhaps regretting their decision to leave Egypt. But as they trusted in the Lord, the miracle unfolded—the sea parted, and they walked on dry land, leaving their fears behind.

In life, we may find ourselves in similar moments, feeling surrounded by chaos and uncertainty. Yet, even in the midst of challenges, God is working. Just as the Israelites experienced their miracle, we too can trust that His plan is unfolding, even when it takes time. Hold on to faith, for your miracle is coming. No matter the storms you face, stay steadfast—God will lead you to victory and reward your trust in Him. Believe in His promises!

Week 52 Friday

It's Payback Time!

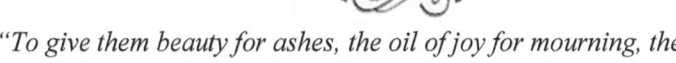

"To give them beauty for ashes, the oil of joy for mourning, the garment of praise for the spirit of heaviness." (Isaiah 61:3, NKJV)

God's promise to give us beauty for ashes is one of hope and restoration. In the Old Testament, ashes symbolized repentance—a visible expression of remorse and humility. People would sit in ashes, roll around in them, or sprinkle them on their heads as an outward sign of their repentance and longing for renewal. But just as those ashes represented turning away from the past, we too must come to a place of release. Letting go of our past mistakes, regrets, wrongdoing, and hurts is essential for stepping into the beauty God has prepared for us.

When we surrender our burdens, God replaces them with blessings that transform us both inwardly and outwardly. He gives us the oil of joy to soothe our mourning and the garment of praise to lift the weight of heaviness. Praise cannot coexist with heaviness—one must give way to the other. Moving on from past hurts, injustices, and negative thoughts is a choice that allows God's restoration to unfold.

It's time to release what holds us back. Payback is coming, not in a negative sense, but through God restoring His best to us. Our history does not define our future; God's plans for us are filled with joy, hope, and assurance. While the past cannot be changed, we can let go of the thoughts that linger and taunt our minds. God's promise of beauty for ashes is His assurance that brighter days are ahead—it's time to claim them!

THE END

Conclusion

These devotionals are a heartfelt accumulation of daily reflections that I've shared with my wife Kathleen, our children, and my Facebook friends. They are inspired by scriptures that reveal God's caring heart and His promises for us. *Coffee with God* represents more than just devotion—it's about cultivating a daily relationship with Him. It's a time to speak to God openly and allow His Word to speak back to us, bringing clarity, reassurance, and peace.

In a world filled with countless voices—our own thoughts, the opinions of family and friends, colleagues, and the endless noise from the world around us—it can be overwhelming to navigate through it all. Yet, amidst this whirlwind, there is one voice that carries true authority: God's voice. His voice is final; His Word has the last say, bringing certainty and guidance to our lives.

Through *Coffee with God*, you are reminded of just how important you are to Him. He longs for you to success, for you to live out the plans and purpose He has lovingly crafted for you. God did not create you to fail. He designed you as someone with value, destined for greatness, and equipped to fulfill the unique calling He has placed on your life.

Take time to tune into His voice and let His truth overshadow the noise of doubt or negativity. You don't need to prove your worth to anyone—God already knows your value and is ready to empower you to thrive. With Him by your side, you can step confidently into the future He has prepared. *Coffee with God* is an invitation to embrace your identity in Him and discover the joy and strength that come from walking in His presence every day. You were made to succeed!

www.ingramcontent.com/pod-product-compliance
Lightning Source LLC
Chambersburg PA
CBHW020418010526
44118CB00010B/310